Play it again
PIANO
BOOK 1

Melanie Spanswick

ED 13935

www.schott-music.com

Mainz • London • Madrid • Berlin • New York • Paris • Prague • Tokyo • Toronto
© 2017 SCHOTT MUSIC Ltd, London

MUSICAL TERMS

Note values are given in the order American-British on their first mention within each section, then American terms alone thereafter.

whole note (semibreve)
half note (minim)
quarter note (crotchet)
eighth note (quaver)
sixteenth note (semiquaver)
thirty-second note (demisemiquaver)

See also the table on page 113

Other terms follow British usage, for example:
bar (Br) = measure (Am)
note (Br) = tone (Am)
semitone (Br) = half step (Am)
stave (Br) = staff (Am)

ED 13935
British Library Cataloguing-in-Publication Data.
A catalogue record for this book is available from the British Library
ISMN 979-0-2201-3761-7
ISBN 978-1-84761-459-9

Cover design by Gary Baker
Book design by Chloë Alexander Design
Music setting by Jeremy Aknai
Photos by Matthew Ward
Back cover photo by Fabrice Rizzato
Printed in Germany S&Co.9369

Contents

From the author

Play it again: Piano is a progressive two-part collection of graded piano pieces for anyone who has played the piano before and wishes to rediscover this fulfilling pastime. This first book starts almost at the beginning, with a look at the musical basics, musicianship and a step-by-step guide on how to learn each piece effectively. *Book 2* follows on progressively from *Book 1*, so you can use *Play it again* whatever your current level of playing ability. You could go straight to *Book 2* if you feel confident enough, but I would always recommend first reviewing the fundamentals of music and piano technique in *Book 1*.

Each book contains carefully selected pieces which gradually increase in difficulty and cover a wide variety of styles and musical periods. By the end of the second book, you should be able to tackle fairly advanced pieces comparable to Grade 8 standard of the leading British exam boards.

For this first book I have selected 28 piano pieces which I hope you will find both interesting and rewarding to play. The book is divided into four sections: Elementary, Late Elementary, Early Intermediate and Intermediate, with the following approximate comparable graded exams (of ABRSM and Trinity College London):

Elementary	Grades 1 to 2
Late Elementary	Grades 2 to 3
Early Intermediate	Grades 3 to 4
Intermediate	Grades 4 to 5

I have included photographs, diagrams and many musical examples to illustrate key aspects of piano technique such as posture, hand positions and basic flexibility, as well as advice on the most effective approaches to practicing. I will show you how to break pieces down in order to help tackle their technical and musical challenges. Once you have completed both books of *Play it again: Piano* you will be able to select, analyse, practice and perform pieces with confidence and enjoy making real progress in your practice sessions.

Melanie Spanswick MMus (RCM), GRSM (Hons), DipRCM, ARCM

www.melaniespanswick.com

How to use *Play it again*

The first part of this book covers the main aspects of piano technique and will serve as a resource to which you can refer when working through the rest of the book. Read these sections thoroughly: good posture, hand positions and movement at the piano are crucial for enjoyable playing. The practice tips and advice will make your time at the keyboard more effective and rewarding; keep these in mind when working through the repertoire.

MUSICAL REMINDERS

The *Theory* section at the end of the book focuses on music notation, the bedrock of all music learning. It may be helpful to review this section before you dive into work on the pieces. The *Theory* section contains some exercises that are designed as note and rhythm 'reminders', and I recommend working at these at the start of each practice session. Key musical terms have been written in **bold** text on their first appearance in the book.

A NOTE ON REPERTOIRE

Each of the four units in *Play it again: Piano – Book 1* (Elementary, Late Elementary, Early Intermediate and Intermediate) features seven piano pieces: a technical study, one or two pieces in a popular style such as jazz, ragtime, blues, rock or Latin, plus an arrangement of a well-known work. The remaining pieces in each unit will help to further your technical and musical progress.

Each piece offers a different focus in terms of technique and musicianship, and is preceded by useful information including preparation tips, practice techniques, tailor-made exercises and ideas for your interpretation.

Piano technique
Posture and hand positions

Sitting correctly at the piano is very important. First make sure your piano stool is at a suitable height (an adjustable stool is ideal); your forearms should be parallel with the keys when your hands rest upon the keyboard. Shoulders and arms should be totally relaxed and in their natural position (not raised). Your hands also need to be in a relaxed, natural position.

Distance from the keyboard is imperative; sit towards the edge of the stool nearest the keyboard so that your feet can rest easily on the floor and support your body as you move (this will also be important when you come to use the foot pedals where the heel of the foot must rest on the floor).

Sit in an upright position without leaning too far forwards or backwards. The hip joint should move freely, so that you are able to reach the whole keyboard with ease.

Align your hands with your elbows and keep your wrists at the same level as your forearm, not raised or falling down.

Resist the urge to sit too near the keyboard as this will affect movement and tone quality.

FLEXIBILITY

It is essential to develop good flexibility when playing the piano. Any rigidity or tension in the upper body will affect dexterity and sound quality. Here are a few tips to help develop freedom of movement in your playing.

Flexibility is sometimes forgotten during practice sessions because our attention is focused elsewhere: reading the music and playing the notes. However, it is extremely beneficial to think about the body and how it moves during performance.

FINGER INDEPENDENCE

Fingers should always work independently of each other and of the muscles in the rest of the hand. Finger joints must be well supported, with each joint fully engaged (as in the first photo below).

Don't let fingers collapse (as demonstrated in the second photo) as this will lead to weaker finger movement.

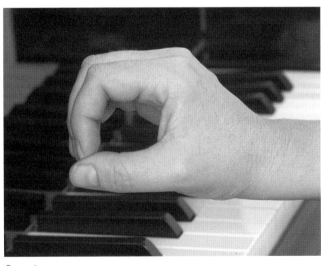

Correct

Incorrect

A 'hooked' finger shape encourages strong finger movement and excellent connection with each key, allowing you to play using the tips of your fingers on each note.

In piano playing, flexibility of the wrists should be considered very important, as any tension or stiffness here usually hinders successful playing. A good rotational movement and wrist flexibility will enable you to move freely around the keyboard. This should ideally be accompanied by a loose forearm, for easy movement up and down the keyboard.

Flexible wrist: exercise 1

Aim for constant movement in the wrist when playing as this will prevent rigidity; avoid holding your wrists in one position, or placing them too high or too low. In order to achieve this, try the following exercise:

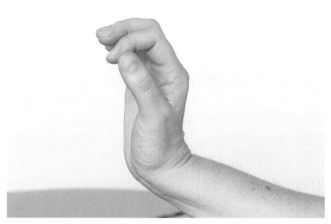

Upwards movement

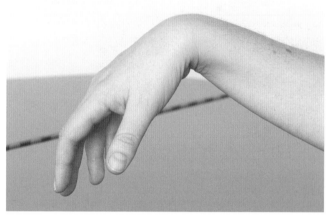

Downwards movement

1 Start by waving your hand from the wrist, first upwards then downwards, with the wrist acting as a hinge. Do this with both hands.

2 Now make a rotational movement as in waving goodbye.

3 Finally, make complete circles in the air, using the wrists as the hinge.

This might seem exaggerated, but it will help you to get used to the movement required to develop complete freedom.

· ·

Flexible wrist: exercise 2

1 At the piano, place your thumb on middle C.

2 Drop your wrist and hand whilst continuing to depress the key (the hand must ideally flop down on the keyboard in order to be really loose).

Rotate wrist between every note

3 The feeling in your hand and wrist should be one of complete relaxation with no tension whatsoever. Some muscle tension is necessary to play a note but, once sounded, try to release all the muscles in the hand.

4 Repeat this technique for the subsequent notes. Each note is held for two beats, so there is plenty of time to move the wrist and the hand between notes.

5 Once you are able to recognise the feeling of relaxation after each note has been played, play the exercise once again but this time rotate the wrist, that is, make a circular motion between each note. This is demonstrated in the photos below, where my wrist makes an anticlockwise circular motion: from a high position (right) to a low position (left).

Now try the same exercise with the left hand:

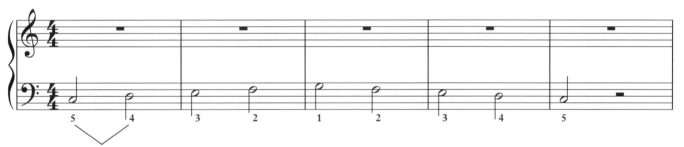

Rotate wrist between notes

Aim to begin practice sessions with these exercises and you'll find your wrists will become gradually more relaxed and supple.

ARM WEIGHT AND SOUND

Being able to produce a good sound is vital as it determines control and evenness. Dynamic range (level of loudness), nuance and articulation (or touch) all become much easier too. The arm can only become really effective once it is free of tension, at which point it can combine with the wrist to produce a warm, rich tone. To achieve this, revisit the exercises above and ensure each finger (and thumb) plays deeply into the key bed.

As you are rotating your wrist, add the weight of your whole arm behind it. You will essentially 'caress' or massage the keys as opposed to playing (or hitting) them directly from above. The resulting sound should be warm, rich, penetrating and deep, and in no way harsh, weedy or meagre (which tends to be the case when the keys are just hit). It is important to listen carefully to the quality of the sound you create during your practice sessions.

Practice
Sight-reading and scales

Sight-reading and scales form a crucial part of successful piano playing. Whilst they might initially appear perfunctory and dull, if worked at regularly and in small doses, the benefits will soon become apparent.

SIGHT-READING

In many ways sight-reading music is similar to learning to read; we gradually become accustomed to what will come next because we have seen the words and phrase patterns many times before. It's the same with music; until common note shapes, patterns and chords have been internalised, slow, careful and thorough preparation is important.

To sight-read fluently is a wonderfully rewarding skill but it requires regular, concentrated work. As it demands a lot of focus, it can be a good way to begin practice sessions.

Tip

With practice you will be able to move through these seven points with increasing speed and confidence. Start with very easy piano music. There are several books dedicated specifically to sight-reading such as the *Piano Sight-Reading* books by John Kember (Schott Music). Above all, have fun experimenting with a range of styles. Ten to fifteen minutes devoted to sight-reading in each of your practice sessions will pay real dividends.

7 sight-reading tips

1 Note the key signature. This indicates which notes (if any) need to be sharpened or flattened throughout the piece. When playing, keep the key signature in mind at all times!

2 The time signature (placed after the key signature at the beginning), will show you how many beats to count (for example, if the piece is in $\frac{3}{4}$ then there will be three quarter note (crotchet) beats in each bar).

3 Play through the music for each hand separately and slowly without following any rhythmic beat, but making a careful note of the fingering. This will help reading skills immeasurably and provides the opportunity to find the notes without the burden of keeping time.

4 Watch out for patterns, both rhythmic and melodic, as well as any scales, arpeggios and chords: these can all act as signposts.

5 To assimilate the rhythm properly, slowly tap the rhythm of the notes with two hands on the piano lid (the right hand tapping the top stave, and the left hand tapping the bottom stave). Count aloud all the time whilst tapping.

6 You are now ready to play with your hands together. Choose a very slow tempo (a third or even a quarter of the intended speed). If the piece consists predominantly of sixteenth notes (semiquavers), then count in sixteenths; if it is mainly eighth notes (quavers), count in eighths and so on. Starting your sight-reading practice material with a slow, steady speed is the key to playing fluently without hesitations. Gradually increase the tempo as you become more confident and fluent; becoming proficient at sight-reading takes time, so be patient!

7 Try not to stop or hesitate; keep on playing through your mistakes – maintaining a steady pulse is more important than playing all the right notes.

SCALES AND ARPEGGIOS

Practicing and mastering scales and arpeggios is of enormous benefit for many reasons, including developing good hand coordination and secure fingering, strengthening fingers, learning all the keys, acquiring evenness and control, learning the geography of the keyboard, and developing a strong sense of rhythm, articulation and speed. Once fluent, scales and arpeggios can improve your sight-reading and will make it easier to learn new pieces.

Scales are sequences of seven notes (in 24 different keys), played up and down the keyboard; arpeggios are sequences of notes constructed from the tonic triad or key chord in all the keys (a chord is a group of notes all sounding at the same time).

7 scales and arpeggios tips

1 Start by practicing very slowly, hands separately, one octave at a time. Grasp the pattern of notes and accidentals within each key before increasing speed or adding more octaves.

2 Check the fingering thoroughly – this is one of the main reasons for practicing slowly. Always remember where the fourth finger occurs in every scale; once this has been internalised you will be much less likely to make errors with fingering.

3 Every note must sound clearly and should be played **legato** (smooth and joined up), unless you're deliberately practicing **staccato** (short and detached) scales. The movement of passing the thumb under the palm of the hand or the hand over the thumb should be smooth, avoiding jerkiness; try to swivel your hand gracefully without tension.

4 To achieve this, practice at a quarter of the intended tempo and use your wrist. Remember to play on your fingertips, playing deep into the key bed to produce a rich but firm tone.

5 A rotational wrist motion can be very helpful in scales and arpeggios. After each note, move the wrist freely and rotate onto the next note (at a slow speed). This promotes flexibility, especially in arpeggios where the **intervals** (distance between the notes) are larger and more varied. As the hands start playing together, wrist motion helps with coordination and accuracy.

6 A steady pulse will facilitate an evenness in your scale playing. Count every note when playing slowly or use a metronome. Listen carefully to your scales, and once you have a good grasp of the pulse and can play all the notes with a full sound and the correct fingerings, you can increase the speed.

7 When playing more quickly, lighten your finger touch to create crisp, even and well-coordinated scales. To do this, the upper body must feel free; the thorough finger preparation combined with flexible hand and wrist motions that you have already practiced should help here.

MUSICIANSHIP AND INTERPRETATION

These aspects can sometimes be forgotten, as a result of your attention being focused on technical demands, but they are areas that shouldn't be overlooked because your interpretation of a piece of music is how you 'put your stamp on it' as a musician. However, the composer will usually have already indicated certain aspects of interpretation in the music such as dynamics (tonal variation), tempo, phrasing and pedalling and it is important that these instructions are followed. We will look at aspects of interpretation and musicianship throughout *Play it again*.

PRACTICE SCHEDULE

It is a good idea to have a realistic practice schedule which is easy to implement. It will encourage regular practice and good progress. Irrespective of how much time you can devote to practicing, aim to include a small amount of sight-reading (5–10 minutes), scale and arpeggio practice (5–10 minutes), as well as time spent working on a few pieces (30–45 minutes). Mixing these elements provides variety (although I would always recommend starting with sight-reading and exercises). 'Little and often' is definitely preferable to one long session once a week.

Tip

The trick to successful practice is the ability to break pieces down, working on them in a logical, focused manner.

We will explore tips for practicing and performing the pieces throughout *Play it again*, and these can be applied to other pieces too, providing a solid foundation for your development as a pianist.

Elementary
Air in D minor

Henry Purcell (1659–1695)

Set up

Key: D minor
Time signature: 3/4
Tempo: Moderato ♩ = 115
Style: Baroque
Piano technique:
- Independence of hands: playing two voices simultaneously

This elegant Baroque piece uses counterpoint – a compositional technique typical of the period in which two or more musical voices (or lines) play together.

PREPARATION

This piece is in D minor, so let's prepare by learning the D minor scale. Note that the harmonic minor version shown below contains a B♮, as indicated by the key signature, and an added C♯. Look at the suggested fingering and before you play, check your posture, ensuring shoulders are down and your arms, hands and wrists are loose.

Work at the arpeggio slowly, hands separately. Strong fingers are developed by playing deeply (and fairly heavily) into each key, playing on the tips of your fingers.

PRACTICE TECHNIQUES

Left-hand practice

First look at the left hand. It contains a quarter note (crotchet) pattern, almost throughout, which keeps the momentum striding forwards. Play the first four bars through slowly, using the suggested fingering. Use a non-*legato* (or 'detached') touch, aiming for a definite 'gap' in the sound between each note. To achieve this allow each finger to leave the note, and roll the hand forwards and upwards, away from the keys.

Now work at the remaining three phrases in the left hand. Watch for the hand and finger position changes which occur at bars 4–5, 8–9 and 10–11; these will need slow, concentrated practice to develop the quick movements required.

Tip

· · · · · · · · · · · · · ·

A phrase is like a musical sentence. Taper off the ends of phrases, and add a very slight break in the sound before the next.

Right-hand practice
Divide the right-hand melody into four-bar sections and work through
these slowly without worrying about the pulse. Watch out for the
fingering and hand-position changes at bars 8–9, 9–10 and 14–15.
Where there are large leaps in the right hand, such as those between
bars 1 and 2, try to maintain flexibility by practicing moving from one
hand position to the next, allowing your wrist to be very loose in-
between. This will help the fluidity, rhythm, and evenness of tone.

The right hand should be played *legato*: each note played very smoothly
and 'joined' to the next. Where the phrase ends (at the end of each
curved line above the notes, so the end of bar 1 in the example above),
the finger or thumb can release the note, making a very slight gap or
'breathing' space before the next phrase.

When you can play the notes in each hand without any hesitation, you
can start to work on the rhythm. First, tap the rhythms on your piano
lid. Subdivide the beat into eighth notes (quavers) (counting 'one-and-
two-and-three-and'), count aloud, and then play along to the pulse you
have established.

· ·

Hands together
When confident, take two bars and play them with hands together at
a quarter of the intended speed. If you make mistakes at first, go even
slower.

Work through the entire piece, two bars at a time. Practice slowly
because playing non-*legato* in the left hand and *legato* in the right hand
at the same time will require concentration, focus and probably much
repetition. Working a beat at a time until hands are really coordinated
also pays dividends.

· ·

INTERPRETATION
Aim for a softer left hand which rises and falls alongside the right
hand's melodic line. Keep it light throughout, occasionally allowing
the right hand to experiment with a deeper touch. The addition of
dynamics (*p* signifies soft, *mp*, moderately soft, and *f*, loud) will help
to contour your interpretation.

- If you find it difficult playing
with hands together, try
working on one beat at a
time.

- Take the first two notes (Ds
in either hand), then play
just to beat two (C♯ in the
right hand, and A in the left),
and stop.

- Practice as many times as is
necessary to assimilate the
pattern and feel comfortable
with the coordination.

- Now try the same thing with
the subsequent beats in the
first few bars, each beat at a
time.

- Once the hands are playing
together fluently and without
any hesitations, play each
four-bar section all the way
through as many times
as is necessary to achieve
accuracy, followed by the
entire piece.

- Gradually increase the
speed.

Air in D minor

ZT 676

Henry Purcell (1659–1695)

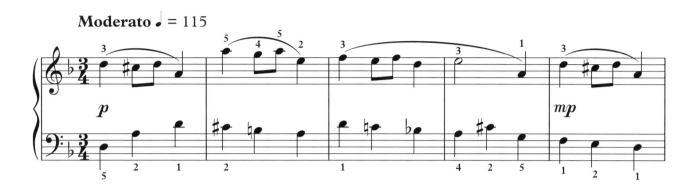

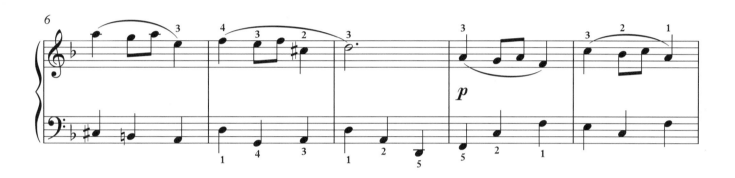

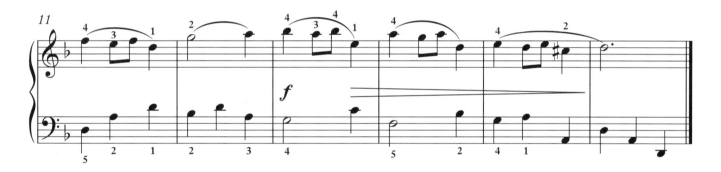

Minuet in G major

Christian Petzold (1677–1733)

This Baroque miniature was formerly attributed to J.S. Bach, but it's now believed to have been written by Christian Petzold. It is in two parts or binary form (A-B) and has a contrapuntal texture.

Set up

Key: G major
Time signature: ¾
Tempo: Moderato ♩ = 126
Style: Baroque
Piano technique:
- Counterpoint: playing two or more musical voices at the same time
- Evenness: eighth note (quaver) passagework

PREPARATION

Start by playing a one octave G major scale (two octaves can be played when you are secure with one octave), then the arpeggio over two octaves. Practice with separate hands at first, ensuring your wrist is flexible and free and able to rotate easily.

Play on your fingertips, and don't forget the F♯ s indicated by the key signature. Play slowly, purposefully and rhythmically, and gradually increase the speed (tempo) as you feel able.

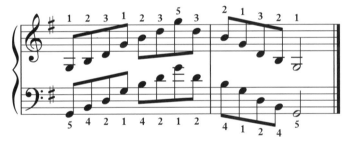

Then try to add your own fingering to the score.

PRACTICE TECHNIQUES

Left-hand practice
Play through the first 16 bars of the left hand; don't worry about the rhythm and instead focus on finding the notes. Say the names of the notes as you play them, reinforcing recognition.

Play the left-hand line again, but this time work on the rhythm, subdividing the beat into eighth notes (quavers) ('one-and-two-and-three-and'), always counting aloud. Ensure the eighth notes at bar 8 are played evenly. Generally the left-hand line needs a *legato* touch, but consecutive quarter notes (crotchets) can be played non-*legato* to coincide with those in the right hand (for example at bar 10).

Right-hand practice
Repeat this process for the right hand, ignoring the **ornament** markings for the time being.

Tip

The opening left-hand chord requires a full sound. Using the suggested fingering, balance the fingers on top of the keys and take the notes down all together at precisely the same time, allowing the chord to sound as one. Whilst the wrist and arm must feel relaxed and flexible, aim to keep the hand in one position, ensuring the fingers (particularly the 5th) are strong and working independently.

Use a non-*legato* touch on the second and third beats of bars 2, 4, 10 and 12 for an effective dance-like 'lift'. Be aware of the various changes in hand position (it can help to practice these separately) and, as with the left hand, count precisely when playing eighth notes to achieve an even sound.

When you can play each line without any errors, in time and with no hesitations, you are ready to put the hands together.

Hands together
Take a bar at a time, working slowly, purposefully, always counting aloud. Practice one bar, and then stop on the first beat of the next. Once four bars have been practiced separately, play them all together. Repeat this process with the final 16 bars. The left hand at bars 25 and 26 will need care as there are essentially two lines of music in one hand. This means that the first B (a half note (minim)) in bar 25 will need to be held right through to the second B (a quarter note), even though a D is sounded above (also played by the left hand).

INTERPRETATION

Ornaments

Ornaments or embellishments are essentially added decorative notes (it is best not to include them too early in your practice as they can tend to disrupt the pulse). This piece includes inverted mordents, a mordent and an appoggiatura.

- **Inverted mordents** and **mordents** are indicated and played as follows, and should be practiced slowly, speeding up only when evenness of touch has been achieved:

- **Appoggiaturas** are written as follows; the small note 'leans' on the main note taking part of its rhythmic value.

Phrases must rise and fall naturally. A suggested **crescendo** (gradually getting louder) from bar 29 to the end, and a very slight **ritenuto** (slowing down) in the final bar, brings this miniature to a close.

Minuet in G major

from **Notebook for Anna Magdalena Bach, BWV Anh. 114**

Christian Petzold (1677–1733)

Moderato ♩ = 126

Andantino

Henri Bertini (1798–1876)

Set up

Key: A minor
Time signature: ¾
Tempo: Andantino ♩ = 104
Style: Early Romantic
Piano technique:

- *Staccato* passagework
- Chords: playing all notes of the chord simultaneously

This beautiful, melancholic piece is a study – a work primarily written to improve a particular aspect of playing, in this case staccato technique and chords.

PREPARATION

Note how the piece is in ternary form (A-B-A), with the first and last sections being very similar. The piece finishes with a brief coda (a concluding passage).

Start your preparation by practicing the A harmonic minor scale and arpeggio. Aim to memorise the scales as you work through each piece.

Chords

When playing a chord, it is important for the notes to sound simultaneously; it can be very easy for them to be split. The best way to avoid this is to allow all fingers to rest on the notes, and practice taking them up and down together, slowly at first, with a loose wrist. The hand and fingers should keep a firm position so all notes can be played at the same moment. Avoid tensing up as you play.

PRACTICE TECHNIQUES

First look at bars 1–16 (bars 9–16 are identical to bars 1–8, which will make learning much quicker). The tempo must be steady throughout; subdivide the beat into eighth notes (quavers) when counting.

Left-hand practice

The first two lines of the left hand are identical, with the same chord patterns. It is crucial to use the correct fingering (written in the score), as this will make each chord that much easier to play. Practice by moving slowly from one chord to the next, making note of the hand-position changes. The jump between bars 3 and 4 is larger than that of the previous bars, and will therefore need a quick finger change. Therefore, programme your mind to switch fingers (and notes) during the rests in bar 3, so you are ready to play the new chord at the right moment (that is, on the 1st beat of the bar).

Practice Notes continue on page 22

Andantino

Op. 137 No. 8

Henri Bertini (1798–1876)

In the third line of the left hand, the chords must be held for the entire bar, moving smoothly from one bar to the next. To achieve this *legato* style keep your fingers firmly on the notes until the last possible moment, then move swiftly to the next chord, aiming for a continuous sound.

Right-hand practice
The right hand is mostly *staccato*. To play this with clarity and vigour, bounce off each note as if it is boiling hot, and then roll the hand and wrist upwards, away from the keyboard. The second note of the first phrase (bar 1, beat 3) is marked **tenuto** (indicated by the line above the note) meaning that it should be held for its full value, with a slight 'leaning', or more marked effect, so try to play it with a little extra care and a deeper sound.

The ornament at bar 5 (and appearing throughout the piece) is an **acciaccatura** or 'crushed note', and it is played like this:

The D should be 'crushed' onto the C as quickly as possible (but must still be audible).

· ·

Hands together
Practice with hands together, taking two bars at a time, very slowly to start with. The two passages marked **forte** (loud), will be best played with a full, warm sound: therefore, prepare to use your wrist flexibly on the chords in the left hand, and use plenty of arm weight in the right.

· ·

INTERPRETATION

Resist the urge to play this piece quickly; it is a beautiful, melancholic ballad.

Contrasts between the opening and closing material (bars 1-16 and bars 25-48) and the shorter middle section (bars 17-24) are important; a much fuller sound would be preferable in the middle section, and also in the coda, bars 41-48.

Observe all dynamic markings carefully, as the success of this piece is down to articulation and tonal variation.

Tip

It can be helpful when practicing ornaments to play the notes slowly and heavily into the key bed producing a full sound.

When played up to speed the finger action can be lighter, producing an even, crisp ornament.

The Sick Doll

Pyotr Ilyich Tchaikovsky (1840 –1893)

Set up

Key: G minor
Time signature: $\frac{2}{4}$
Tempo: Moderato ♩= 69
Style: Romantic
Piano technique:

- 'Voicing': the balance of sound between the bass and melody parts
- Tonal colour: creating an expressive performance

This poignant piece from Tchaikovsky's Album for the Young *is in simple, duple time ($\frac{2}{4}$) and comprises two sections (binary form).*

PREPARATION

Practice the scale and arpeggio of G minor, which contains B♭, E♭ and F♯ (the sharpened seventh note of the harmonic minor scale).

PRACTICE TECHNIQUES

There are three distinct layers of sound here: the bass line and middle part (which form the accompaniment) and the melody. These layers require careful 'voicing' or a balancing of sound between the hands.

Top line: Middle line: Bottom line:

Right-hand practice
Work at the first 16 bars of the right hand; each quarter note (crotchet) in the first line will benefit from a *cantabile* or 'singing' tone, requiring sonority and colour. The *tenuto* markings over every note indicate that there should be a slight 'leaning' on each, adding poignancy.

Use a flexible wrist and arm-weight to produce a full sound; play into the key bed (right to the bottom of the key), rather than sliding over the surface.

Aim to join each note of the second line in a smooth *legato* manner and add the dotted quarter note underneath very softly, but rhythmically. The whole right-hand line can be worked at in this way.

Left-hand practice
The left-hand writing is mostly in two parts. Look at the bottom part, the bass, first using the suggested fingering. Be sure to use a deeper touch for the quarter notes in the second line, which are marked tenuto.

Once you can play the bass line evenly you can turn your attention to the middle part: the two-note dotted quarter note chords. This will benefit from separate practice; play the two notes slowly, so they can be easily located and sound simultaneously. Pressing the keys fully down to the key bed will help. Once secure, put both left-hand parts together.

Hands together
Once you can play each hand with ease you can start practicing hands together. Rhythmic precision is important, and listening will be crucial too, as the melody should be foregrounded with the other parts accompanying. Try playing all three parts powerfully, then pull back and gently 'stroke' the left-hand chords and bass line to produce a lighter, atmospheric ambience. A slight *ritenuto* or slowing down in the last four bars will enhance the sorrowful mood.

INTERPRETATION

Aim to use a different colour or sonority for each four bar phrase, particularly at the beginning of a phrase; this way your sound will be constantly varied. The end of each phrase generally tails off requiring a slight **diminuendo** (getting softer), with the exception of bars 35–41, which must *crescendo* to bar 38 and then die away to **pianissimo** (very soft) at the end.

Tip

Be sure to experiment with a variety of dynamics and colour, in particular by highlighting the forte B♭ at bar 21 (right hand), adding a yearning, expressive quality (possibly depicting the Doll's unfortunate plight).

The Sick Doll

Op. 39 No. 7

Pyotr Ilyich Tchaikovsky (1840 –1893)

Salut d'Amour

Edward Elgar (1857–1934)

This is a delightful arrangement of a salon piece (a light, occasional work) originally written for violin and piano.

Set up

Key: C major
Time signature: 2/4
Tempo: Andantino ♩= 76
Style: Late Romantic
Piano technique:
• *Cantabile*: playing in a singing style

PREPARATION

Start by working at the scale and arpeggio of C major to warm-up the fingers and familiarise yourself with the key of this piece.

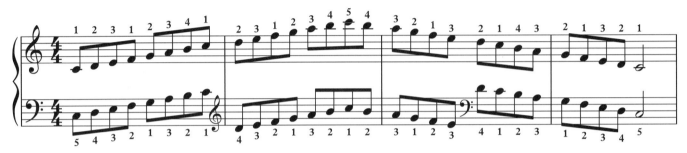

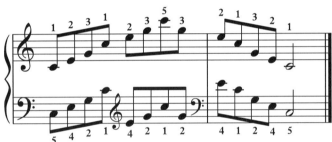

PRACTICE TECHNIQUES

Left-hand practice
The left hand can be 'blocked out' for ease of learning. This means playing groups of notes as a chord (using the same fingerings as if playing the notes as written), like this (left hand: bars 1–7):

Once you have played through the whole piece in this way, play it again as written. The lower line must be very smooth (*legato*), and should be played as evenly as possible. The upper line can be soft, but must be rhythmically accurate. As usual, counting will pay dividends here; ensure the 'offbeat' or **syncopated** middle part is audible and precise.

Right-hand practice
The right hand requires a *cantabile* (singing) sound. Observe the phrasing; add more sound at the tops of phrases but keep in mind that this is an intimate piece. At bar 14, Elgar has indicated **dolce** (sweetly); this is the key to a convincing interpretation.

Tip

Syncopation: where the rhythmic accent is displaced, typically onto what would otherwise be the weaker beat.

'Free wrist' exercise

This exercise helps develop a free, relaxed wrist which will enable you to achieve the warm, rich sound required.

- Play a single note (using your third finger), and as you strike the key, drop the wrist completely, allowing the weight of your arm to drop too, supporting the finger. Your fingers should be completely relaxed and arms almost like a dead weight, feeling as though resting by your side.
- Use your finger pad and 'caress' the key, using the weight of your hand and arm, resisting the urge to 'hit' from above. You can rest the finger pad on the note before it is played, so when the key is depressed, the power comes from the wrist, arm and torso, producing a rich, full sound.
- Apply this technique to the whole right-hand part (using all suggested fingerings).
- Now practice hands together, two bars at a time.

INTERPRETATION

Experiment with a little **rubato** (a slight slowing down or speeding up) to add expression. It could be used at bar 13 where the top As need a little more time to sound, providing an expressive flavour, and from bar 16 onwards (especially during the repeat). This technique needs careful use, however, as too much *rubato* will disrupt the rhythm and sound musically inappropriate.

The sustaining pedal

Use the sustaining (right) pedal to enhance your performance, adding a rich resonance.
- Let your foot rest on the pedal, with the heel of your foot firmly on the floor.
- Take the pedal down where *Ped.* is indicated on the score, and up where the line is broken with an inverted 'V' marking (see the example below).
- Where there are no pedal markings (as in this piece) you'll need to decide where to use the pedal. Experiment by listening carefully ensuring minimal 'smudging' of harmonies (too much pedal can result in a very resonant and unclear sound).
- In this piece applying the pedal on every quarter note (crotchet) beat is appropriate.

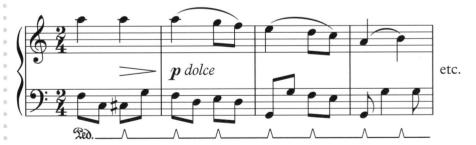

- The sustaining pedal is the most frequently used of the piano pedals. The others are the *una corda* pedal on the left (which softens, or mutes the sound) and the middle or *sostenuto* pedal (which sustains selected notes whilst allowing others to remain unaffected). The *sostenuto* pedal does not appear on all pianos, and is on some pianos replaced by a 'practice' pedal, which mutes the strings significantly for quiet practice.

Salut d'Amour

Op. 12

Edward Elgar (1857–1934)

Calypso

John Kember (b.1935)

Set up

Key: F major
Time signature: 4/4
Tempo: Rhythmically ♩ = 132
Style: Contemporary/World
Piano technique:
- Rhythm: developing an understanding of syncopation

This lively, rhythmic piece is in ternary form (A-B-A), with a texture consisting of melody and accompaniment.

PREPARATION

Practice the F major scale and arpeggio so that the key becomes familiar.

PRACTICE TECHNIQUES

Right-hand practice

The calypso style is characterised in this piece by its syncopated rhythms and by the melody's combination of short, slurred phrases and *staccato* notes.

Look at the first two bars. Once the notes are secure, tackle the rhythm. Keep time by developing a regular pulse (like a ticking clock – a metronome set to an eighth note (quaver) beat may help) and counting in eighth notes, as shown below:

Rhythmically

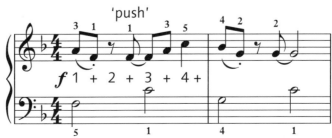

The 'drop roll' technique

Work at a 'drop roll' technique for the short phrases (such as bar 1, beat 1 between notes A and F), where the wrist drops whilst playing the first note and then rolls upwards as the second note is struck.

Dropping into the note

Rolling up after the note has been struck

Rolling away from the note

As you roll off the second note in each short phrase of the calypso, be sure to play it **staccato**.

The eighth note (quaver) on beat two will benefit from a very slight 'push' even though not marked in the score; the 'off-beat' effect will add a syncopated Caribbean flavour. At the beginning of bar 2, the 4th finger must play a B♭. In order to ensure the finger is ready to play this black note, encourage the wrist to guide the finger over the note at the end of bar 1, moving it slightly forward in preparation. Keep your fingers close to the keys where possible to assure accuracy.

In bars 9–12 the right hand plays a series of two-note chords. The gap or distance between the lower and upper notes in each chord is called an interval. The chord in bar 9 has an interval of a sixth, followed by two fifths and a third. Aim to play the two notes of each chord absolutely together.

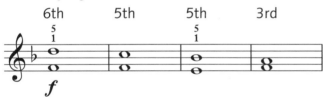

Left-hand practice
The left hand takes the melody in the third line (bars 9–12) so apply the same ideas for playing a syncopated phrase as for the right hand. The left hand half notes (minims) (which appear in lines 1, 2 and 4) should ideally be soft and light, supporting the melody. For a powerful climax, include **fortissimo** (very loud) Fs in the last bar.

INTERPRETATION

Experiment with contrasts of sound for every two-bar phrase. Aim for a smooth, soft accompaniment in the left hand, which will allow the melody to shine.

Calypso

John Kember (b.1935)

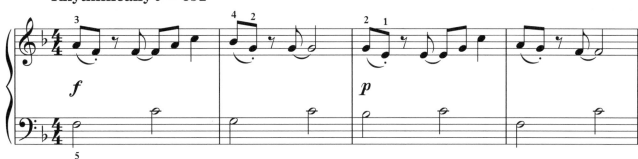

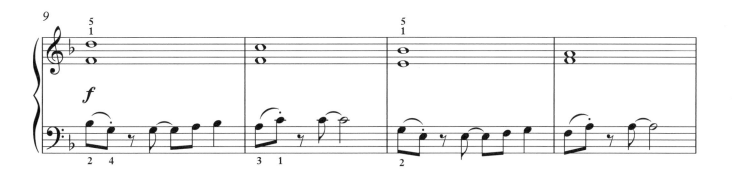

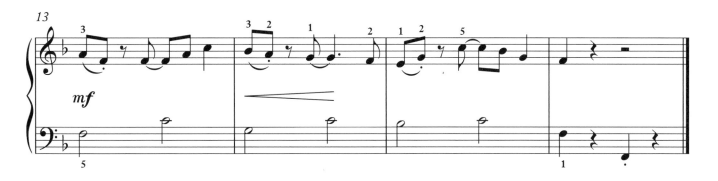

Super Duck

Elena Cobb (b. 1965)

Super Duck is fun, satisfying to play, and provides the perfect introduction to improvisation – a feature particularly of jazz music where the musicians play spontaneously without following written notation.

Set up

Key: C major
Time signature: 4/4
Tempo: Swing eighth notes (quavers) ♩ = 116
Style: Jazz
Piano technique:
- Rhythm: swung eighth notes
- Improvisation on the blues scale

PREPARATION

In this piece we will use the so-called swing style which involves pairs of notes (usually eighth notes (quavers)) being played with a triplet feel, like this:

Swing rhythm exercise

Play through the examples in the rhythmic chart below, tapping each hand on the lid of the piano. Start slowly, making sure you master each example before moving on.

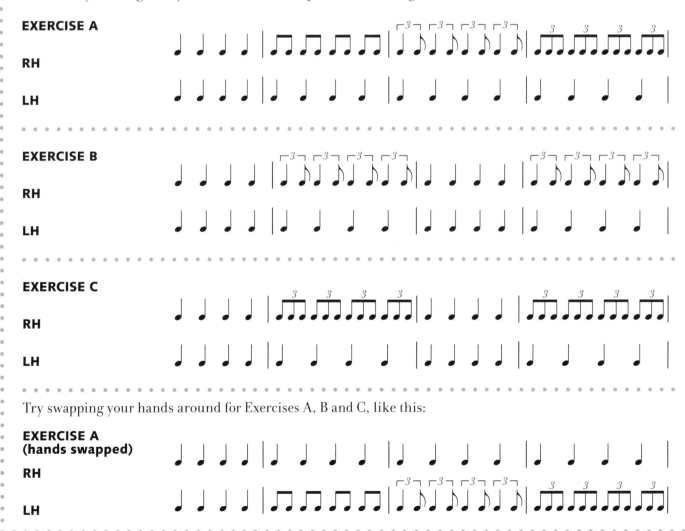

Try swapping your hands around for Exercises A, B and C, like this:

When playing swing triplets, aim to play the quarter notes (crotchets) in each triplet with a deeper tone and the eighth notes slightly lighter. This helps to convey the relaxed swing feel.

PRACTICE TECHNIQUES

Left-hand practice

The left hand is almost entirely made up of intervals of a fifth and sixth (a five- or six-note gap). Work slowly, finding the notes and their positions, adding your own fingering, before playing through counting to a quarter note beat.

Right-hand practice

The right hand features an improvisation section in bars 15–26. First play the stemless notes written in the first treble stave in bar 15 – these form the blues scale on C. Experiment with these notes (using the first four notes to begin with: C E♭ F and F♯, getting used to the shape). Play them in any order, making up your own rhythmic patterns, and becoming accustomed to the jazzy sound. When you feel ready you can try improvising in the right hand using the notes of this scale; play them in any pattern or rhythm and it will nearly always sound good!

Super Duck is based on the **12-bar blues** which is a simple three-chord progression using (in the key of C) C, F and G major triads. This is explained in more detail on page 55 (*Jump Shuffle* by Tim Richards). After assimilating this pattern, you can play the improvisation section in *Super Duck* confidently, letting your imagination run wild! Remember that each bar has four beats.

Tip

. . . .

Triplets and swing: A triplet is a group of three notes of equal duration played within the time normally taken by two notes of the same kind. These are usually indicated by a '3' sign above or below the notes, but in jazz and popular styles, the swing feel is often written at the beginning in the metronome marking, in this case 'swing eighth notes (quavers)', or 'triplet feel' in the case of *Jump Shuffle* by Tim Richards (page 57).

INTERPRETATION

Consider playing bars 15–26 (the solo section) more than once: perhaps once as written, followed by one or two improvised solos. To finish, play a **tremolo** (or a rapid 'trembling' effect) on the final Cs. This means playing octaves (an eight-note interval) at the end, as notated below.

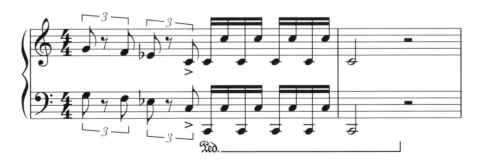

When you're confident, you can speed it up.

Super Duck

Elena Cobb (b. 1965)

End solo

King William's March

Jeremiah Clarke (1674–1707)

This march was written for William of Orange, King of England. Its 16 bars (set in four-bar phrases) are **through-composed**, *meaning the music is non-sectional and not overly repetitive.*

PREPARATION

Begin by practicing a D major scale and arpeggio.

Set up

Key: D major
Time signature: 𝄴
('common time') = 4/4
Tempo: March tempo ♩ = 126
Style: Baroque
Piano technique:
- Keeping a steady pulse
- Touch: contrasting *staccato* and *legato* passagework
- Quick movement around the keyboard

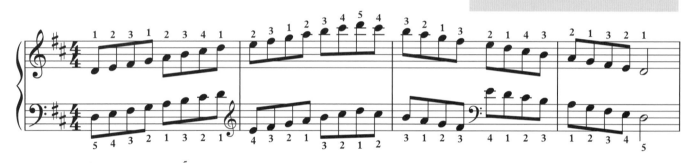

PRACTICE TECHNIQUES

Work on each hand separately, taking a four-bar phrase at a time.

Left-hand practice
The contrast between *staccato* and *legato* passagework is very important in this piece. Ensure each phrase is played *legato*. The repeated Ds (for example in bars 1–3) are marked *tenuto* and should be held for their full duration, with a slightly deeper sonority, as though 'leaning' into the keys.

The left-hand movement in bars 9–10, 13 and 14 needs careful work; when playing the octaves at bars 9 and 10 use a lateral wrist motion (where the wrist moves to the side as opposed to a rotational movement) to reach the notes easily.

At bars 13 and 14, block out the notes (finding and playing all the notes in the bar all together at once) in order to master the patterns.

Tip

In beat 4 of bars 1, 5 and 9, the right hand 5th finger must play an F♯. This can be inconvenient, so take each passage out of context. Guide a relaxed wrist slightly to the right, providing more support to the 5th finger (as it is often the weakest). Use the fingertip, encouraging the finger to 'stand', so it appears 'hooked'. Once the 5th fingertip can make a proper connection with the key, finding the necessary 'grip' needed to secure repeated accuracy won't be a problem.

Right-hand practice

The opening right-hand motif (shown below) is repeated in many forms, and requires a majestic feel and large sound in keeping with the style of a march. Use a separate movement on each of the first three notes in the right hand to achieve the full sound, accents and *staccato* required. As you play the note, allow the wrist to drop and then rise, rolling forward after the note has been sounded.

- Pay particular attention to the pulse and rhythm. Count carefully, subdividing the beats (it may even be helpful to write this into the score in between the staves).

- Take note of the dotted quarter note (crotchet)/ eighth note (quaver) rhythms at bars 8 and 16. These will need to be placed precisely, so count each beat out loud.

- At bars 2–3, 6–7 and 12–13 different hand positions and fingerings are necessary; you will need to pick your hand up completely and move it to a different part of the keyboard. Practice moving quickly and with precision. Isolate each area, and play at double the speed (always moving flexibly) until secure; then when playing at the normal tempo, the jumps will feel comfortable.

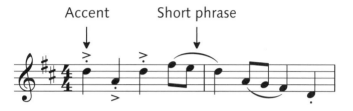

An **accent mark** (as shown over the first three notes in the example above), places emphasis on a particular note and, when added to the *staccato*, will convey drama, colour and grandeur. However, resist the urge to 'snatch' these notes; aim to think of the *staccato* and accented articulation as a crisp, short, richly pronounced quarter note (crotchet), which should ideally last *nearly* the whole quarter note beat.

The two short *legato* phrases in bars 1–2 should be played with a 'drop-roll' movement (as described in *Calypso*, page 30), dropping the wrist on the first note and rolling up after the third.

· ·

Hands together

Once each hand is secure, practice small sections with both hands together, and ensure plenty of dynamic contrast between phrases.

· ·

INTERPRETATION

This piece requires very little sustaining pedal, but adding a small amount at the end of phrases will help to sustain the sound. Experiment at bars 4, 8 (just the last half note (minim) beat), 12 (the last half note beat), and bar 16 (pedal both half note beats here). Try to depress the pedal a fraction after playing a note to avoid blurring the changing harmonies.

King William's March

Jeremiah Clarke (1674–1707)

Allegro in B-flat major

Wolfgang Amadeus Mozart (1756–1791)

Set up

Key: B♭ major
Time signature: 2/4
Tempo: Allegro ♩ = 104
Style: Classical
Piano technique:

- Phrasing: the 'drop roll' technique
- Articulation: non-*legato* and short *legato* phrases

This elegant Allegro *by Mozart is in binary form (A–B), with a melody-plus-accompaniment texture.*

PREPARATION

Begin by working at the scale and arpeggio of B♭ major, which contains B♭ and E♭. This scale requires a different fingering pattern; start with the second finger in the right hand and the third in the left hand, and make a note of where the fourth finger falls in both hands before practicing slowly.

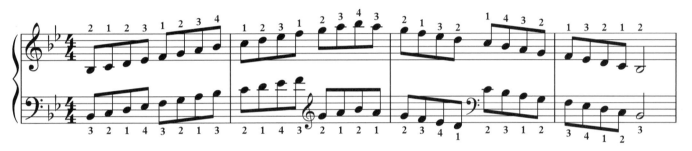

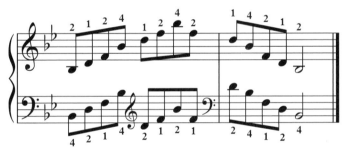

PRACTICE TECHNIQUES

Left-hand practice
Take time locating all the left-hand notes with their correct fingerings. You can add your own fingerings here if you prefer.

The left-hand requires a mixture of *legato* (very smooth) and non-*legato* (slightly longer than staccato, but still detached), touches. Play the quarter notes (crotchets) and dotted quarter notes with a *tenuto* effect; holding them until the very last moment and then lifting the finger before playing the next note. Eighth notes (quavers) can be articulated non-*legato*. A slightly detached effect will tie in nicely with that of the right hand.

Right-hand practice
The right hand features short phrase patterns and requires a precise non-*legato* touch. It has a large range, so the hand needs to move across the keyboard swiftly and economically. Practice slowly until you have fully mastered the note patterns and, more importantly, the movements needed to play them correctly every time.

Look at the opening arpeggio figure (bars 1–2, and echoed throughout).
Allow a wide stretch from the F down to the D and B♭. The F can be
non-*legato*, leaping onto the D; ensure the fifth finger is well supported
by the arm and wrist to produce a big sound at the opening. Use the
'drop-roll' technique to play the slurred couplets, allowing the wrist
and hand to drop onto the D, rolling forward and up as the B♭ is played,
leaving a slight gap before playing the next phrase pattern, an A and C.

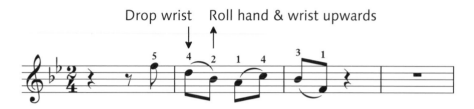

The repeated 'answering' phrase from bar 2 (last eighth note) to bar
6 (first beat) should be played semi-*staccato*, bouncing on each note
to create a warm, full sound. Apply these techniques to the rest of the
right-hand part.

Aim to play the *acciaccatura* at bars 9 and 27 as follows:

Hands together
Once you can play the hands separately with no hesitations, practice
with both hands together in short phrases, counting continuously. The
metronome is a friend of the Classical style, so work with it slowly at
first, gradually increasing the speed.

INTERPRETATION
Dynamics play a crucial role in helping to illuminate the 'echo' effects
(as in bar 2 (last last eighth note) to bar 6 (first beat)). Remember to play
both repeats for the full Mozart experience!

Allegro in B-flat major

KV 3

Wolfgang Amadeus Mozart (1756–1791)

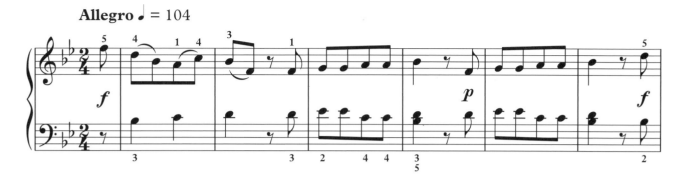

Soldier's March

Robert Schumann (1810–1856)

This sprightly march is from Schumann's Album for the Young, *which he composed in 1848 for his three daughters. It is in binary form (with both sections repeated), and has a chordal texture.*

PREPARATION

Work at the G major scale and arpeggio (see page 16).

In preparation, try playing the right-hand top line or melody without the rest of the texture (that is, the other notes), like this:

etc.

Use the correct fingering (which will be employed when the other right-hand notes are added), and focus on colouring and contouring the melody.

PRACTICE TECHNIQUES

Left-hand practice

The left hand provides the backbone for the right hand, and contains several quick position changes, therefore give it a considerable amount of focused work. Fingering is crucial so try to adhere to the suggestions provided.

In bar 6, the left hand jumps from the thumb (a C on beat 1) to the fourth finger (a B on beat 2). Practice this with quick, repeated movements until you can play it at a much faster speed than required for the piece.

The second half of the piece, bars 9–24, is characterised by contrasting dynamics; bars 9–10 are forte whereas 11–12 are immediately **piano** (quiet or 'soft'), requiring good control of nuance and expression.

Right-hand practice

Now turn to the right hand, which contains two-note chords almost throughout. Observe the note patterns and how the fingers need to move from one chord to the next. These will benefit from slow, careful practice, particularly bars 11–12, 15–16 and 23–24.

Tip

Counting

The best way to tackle rhythm and pulse is to subdivide the beat.
- In this piece, aim to count in sixteenth notes (semiquavers), counting aloud as you play (this is really important, so as to not rush the sixteenth notes, placing them properly).
- Aim to release each eighth note (quaver) swiftly, taking note of the following rest and reinforcing the 'march' feel.

Hands together

Once the notes have been located, start practicing with hands together at a very slow tempo (about a quarter of the intended speed); work in four-bar phrases, breaking down each phrase, ensuring complete fluency in one section before moving on to the next.

Because we are aiming at producing a warm sound played without hesitation it's important to work in sections, gradually building up accuracy and eventually using a metronome. Keep the pulse even and very regular, without any hesitations, and avoid rushing the quarter notes (crotchets) before the leaps onto the chords at bars 11 and 15.

INTERPRETATION

Pay special attention to the colour and tone of the very top line. Turn the right hand slightly by moving the wrist and arm outwards (to the right, away from the body) when playing. This will support the naturally weaker fourth and fifth fingers, allowing them to play with greater power on their tips (rather than the flat part of the finger). By using finger power, and playing deep into the keys, the melody will ring out, and in turn the lower part of each chord (usually played with the thumb or second finger), can be voiced softly and lightly.

Tip

The sustaining pedal will provide resonance and soul to your performance. Aim to add it to bars 9–10, 13–14 and 21–24, taking the pedal down on the first and second beat of the bars, clearing it swiftly. Give each dotted eighth note (quaver)- sixteenth note (semiquaver) pair a slight push or accent on the first beat and articulate the sixteenth notes with clarity and crispness.

Soldier's March

Op. 68 No. 2

Robert Schumann (1810–1856)

Allegro non troppo

Cornelius Gurlitt (1820 –1901)

Set up

Key: D minor

Time signature: 𝄵

Tempo: Allegro non troppo

♩ = 100

Style: Romantic

Piano technique:

- Chordal control: repeated right-hand chords
- Left-hand *cantabile*

The melody is played by the left hand in this piece, with the right hand supplying accompanying chords.

PREPARATION

Revisit the scale and arpeggio of D minor (see page 13). Finding the note patterns and fingerings should be relatively easy; returning to scales and exercises previously studied will, hopefully, remind you of the progress you have made.

Tonal colour

In order to experiment with tonal colour – which is a necessary feature of this piece – work at the exercise below (built from bars 2–5 of the right hand).

ppp   *pp*   *p*   *mp*   *mf*   *f*   *ff*

Take each chord up and down slowly, increasing the tone by using a flexible wrist movement to gradually add more weight from your arm. The balance of hand and fingers will be important when playing two notes simultaneously for many bars.

PRACTICE TECHNIQUES

Left-hand practice

The melody is given to the left hand in this piece. First, slowly run through all the notes and fingerings (don't worry about the rhythm at this stage). Notice that several phrases have several hand position changes; be prepared to move swiftly for these. One way of doing this is to practice moving extremely quickly from one position to another, taking care to maintain flexibility.

Cantabile playing

The following exercise will help to develop *cantabile* playing (in a singing style), which is required from the left hand throughout this piece.

- Once you can confidently play the notes, allow your wrist to be completely loose.
- Playing slowly, allow your wrist to drop freely in between beats whilst still physically holding onto the keys (your arm, wrist and hand should feel relaxed, heavy and flexible and in no way tense or tight). A full sound and singing tone will come from the added arm-weight and by cushioning each note as it is played (as opposed to sliding over the key).
- Aim to shape each phrase whilst still adhering to the dynamics.

Right-hand practice

The right hand has accompanying eighth note (quaver) chords throughout. Two things are particularly important here: use the suggested fingering for a *legato* approach, and make sure the chords are played evenly. Rhythmically, counting between beats or subdividing will help. Tonally, practice taking each chord up and down slowly, finding the key bed (rather like the 'biting point' of a car clutch!), and once found, ensure the notes are played exactly together and not split. Vary the tone to fit with the left-hand melody line; the slower the attack, the softer the tone. The right hand must always be subordinate to the left hand in this piece.

Tip

When increasing the volume resist the temptation to rush!

INTERPRETATION

A slight *ritenuto* (slowing down) at the end is all that is needed in terms of rubato. The sustaining pedal will be a welcome addition if played with every left-hand half note (minim) beat. A soft right hand will create an appropriate mysterious character.

Allegro non troppo

Op. 82 No. 65

Cornelius Gurlitt (1820 –1901)

Study No. 25

Ludvig Schytte (1848–1909)

A study is a piece that focuses on a particular aspect of piano technique, to help master specific technical skills. In this study, the focus is on chords.

Set up

Key: B♭ major

Time signature: ¢

Tempo: Moderato ma deciso
♩ = 108

Style: Romantic

Piano technique:

- Chords: balancing the notes of each chord
- Rhythm: keeping a steady pulse

PREPARATION

Revisit the scale and arpeggio of B♭ major (see page 39).

Now let's examine the chord structures. The study is constructed of fairly straightforward chord progressions, and there are many repeats, for example bars 3 and 4 are exactly the same as bars 1 and 2.

Blocking out the chords as below makes it easy to see patterns, shapes, fingering and musical direction, as well as where to move.

PRACTICE TECHNIQUES

Left-hand practice

The note pattern in the left hand is almost identical throughout. When practicing, count all the beats out loud; there are many rests in the left hand, so ensure you don't ignore or skip them.

Practice using a full tone to begin with then, when secure, lighten your touch, keeping the left-hand chords softer than those of the right hand.

Leaps

The following exercise will help in tackling leaps. The leaps in this piece can be found in bars 9–16 in the left hand; these need not be an issue as they are essentially similar note patterns to the first part of the piece.

- For practice purposes, move from chord to chord more quickly than is actually necessary, and focus on the chord shape and fingering. Repeat until you've grasped the size of each leap.
- It can be beneficial to practice a much larger leap than written, so instead of jumping one octave, try a two octave leap, like this:

- When you return to the original, it will feel much more comfortable.
- Change patterns regularly by practicing different sections of the piece and use a free wrist with very light arm movements.
- Once mastered, focus on lightening your touch, adding speed. Aim to play these leaps until they become second nature; then when you add the right hand your focus can be solely on the melodic line.

Legato chords

The right-hand part demands a smooth, legato sound when playing chord progressions. Use the following exercise to practice this technique.

- Play just the top line of the first bar (B♭ to A) completely legato, then the middle line (F to E♭), also playing as legato as possible. Finally, practice joining the two thumbs evenly.
- When joining the F to the E♭ and the D to the C (with thumbs), it will be necessary to hold the first note until the very last moment, moving quickly from one note to the next, creating an illusion of *legato* and also matching the sound.
- Now play both chords as they are written, joining them smoothly.
- Apply this practice technique to the rest of the first line (and the whole piece).
- Practice using a heavy tone, then when fluent, lighten the touch and always join the top line carefully. Keep the melody line bright, with the remaining parts of the chord light and soft.

Right-hand practice
Use the correct fingering to enable easy movement between the chords – this is key to mastering an even tone and rhythm.

Hands together
Counting out loud is really helpful when practicing with both hands together. Whilst the right hand needs a greater tone than the left, every note must be given its full value so resist the urge to rush with the left hand. Try counting in eighth notes (quavers) to secure a firm, steady, and precise pulse.

INTERPRETATION

Each two-bar phrase begins brightly, getting softer towards the end of the phrase, as shown below. The final phrase is the only one requiring a full sonority at the end.

Start by practicing slowly, and raise the metronome marking when secure.

Study No. 25

from **25 Melodious Studies, Op. 108**

Ludvig Schytte (1848–1909)

Maple Leaf Rag

Scott Joplin (1867/8–1917), arranged by Melanie Spanswick (b. 1969)

Set up

Key: G major
Time signature: 2/4
Tempo: March tempo ♩ = 100
Style: Ragtime
Piano technique:
- Syncopation: playing in a Ragtime style
- Articulation: accents

This well-known piece is by the 'King of Ragtime', Scott Joplin. **Ragtime** *is a style of music characterised by a syncopated (off-beat) melody and an accented accompaniment.*

PREPARATION

Revisit the G major scale and arpeggio (page 16) to familiarise yourself with the key of this piece. Play through the *Maple Leaf Rag*, hands separately, noting all fingerings (and adding some, where you feel it is necessary).

PRACTICE TECHNIQUES
Left-hand practice

Left-hand eighth note (quavers)

- In preparation for playing the left-hand eighth note pattern, it can be helpful to play repeated notes in order to grasp positions and fingering. The example below illustrates the first few bars.

- If you play this pattern throughout (making sure your wrist and arm are free of tension at all times), it will help note-learning and ensure rhythmic precision, by increasing awareness of rhythmic placing.

The left hand should be played non-*legato* throughout. Work through a bar at a time, blocking out whole bars as shown in the example below. Aim to play each note pattern as a chord or group of notes (one per bar) using the intended fingering:

Rhythm is crucial in a work such as this; the pulse must remain stable in order that the melody's syncopation (or off-beat pattern) is 'placed' correctly, providing the jazz-like feel. The wrist should remain very flexible in order to keep the note changes accurate and the articulation 'snappy', short, sharp and punchy.

Practice Notes continue on page 54

Maple Leaf Rag

Scott Joplin (1867/8–1917)

arr. Melanie Spanswick (b. 1969)

March tempo ♩ = 100

Play it again: Piano – Book 1

Right-hand practice

The right hand's sixteenth notes (semiquavers) can all be *legato*. Keep the arm and wrist flexible whilst moving from one section to another, for example at the two-octave jump in bar 12.

When playing in sections always count aloud and use a metronome. Every beat must be accounted for without any sense of rushing or slowing down. Once you have mastered this the hands can be practiced together.

Tip

The '8' with a dotted line in bars 12–14 and 28–30 means you should play the right hand an octave higher than written.

Hands together

Work through the piece in small sections. Experiment by playing the right hand as written and the left hand as chords (this could also work the other way around).

Small accents (or 'pushes') on certain beats in the left and right hands will enhance the ragtime flavour. Experiment with the suggested accents in the following example, aiming to place every note carefully (to aid counting, the sixteenth note beat has been added in between the staves):

INTERPRETATION

Try practicing with a deep touch, then lighten it a little (although not too much as this style of music is best played with a strident swagger and plenty of sonority). Use the sustaining pedal sparingly!

Jump Shuffle

Tim Richards (b. 1952)

Set up

Key: C major
Time signature: 4/4
Tempo: ♩ = 108 (triplet feel)
Style: Blues
Piano technique:
- Swing: playing with a triplet feel
- 12-bar blues progression

Jump Shuffle is a great little jazzy piece that uses the 12-bar blues chord progression, and should be played with a triplet feel.

PREPARATION

Revisit the C major scale and arpeggio (page 26) before beginning to learn this piece.

Jump Shuffle is structured around the 12-bar blues progression. Let's look at the chord structure:

The same pattern is repeated several times in the left hand, (until the last bar), but is based on the different chords. This is typical of the Blues and Boogie piano style. It's worth noting the pattern of chords in the 12-bar blues progression: 4 bars on C, 2 bars on F, 2 more bars on C, then G and F for a bar each before returning to C for 2 bars.

Block each bar out and play the chords as a group (as suggested in the above example); this can be a very useful, quick method of surveying the chord structure and learning notes.

PRACTICE TECHNIQUES

Hands together

Practice the chord pattern keeping a very steady beat (particularly in the left hand). Use a metronome to help keep the pulse. The left hand should ideally be played *legato*, whilst the right hand can be played short and non-*legato*.

Once secure, play the right-hand chords as part of a triplet to give a **swing** feel, like this:

Counting in triplets can help here. Ensure this pattern sounds relaxed with a real 'groove'.

The second half of this piece (known in jazz terminology as the 'second chorus'), continues the swing feel, with all eighth notes (quavers) played with the same triplet pattern.

. . . .

INTERPRETATION

Pay special attention to the accents in the right-hand melody, which are often halfway through the **upbeat** (the beat immediately preceding the first beat of the bar, or **downbeat**) at the end of each bar. The important accents have ties over the barline, for example in bars 14–15 as shown below. These require an extra 'push', without upsetting the regular pulse set by the left hand.

Be sure to use the suggested fingering at bars 16 and 20, in the left-hand 'run-ups' where a chromatic pattern occurs before a change of harmony.

Jump Shuffle

Tim Richards (b. 1952)

♩ = 108 (triplet feel)

Second chorus

Left-hand run up

Left-hand run up

from **Improvising Blues Piano** by Tim Richards, Schott ED 12504

Early Intermediate
Prelude in C minor

Johann Sebastian Bach (1685–1750)

A **prelude** is a short piece often acting as an introduction to a **suite** of pieces. As is common in Baroque music, very little information is written in the score; I would suggest Allegro for the tempo.

Set up

Key: C minor
Time signature: ¾
Tempo: Allegro ♩ = 88–92
Style: Baroque
Piano technique:
- Articulation: sixteenth note (semiquaver) passagework
- Rhythm: keeping an even pulse

PREPARATION

Let's begin with the scale and arpeggio of the key of the piece, C minor. Whilst the key signature contains three flats (B♭, E♭ and A♭), the fingering is the same as that of C major. The arpeggio will be particularly useful for this piece, as both the left hand and right hand passages are often built around the key chord.

PRACTICE TECHNIQUES

Right-hand practice

This piece is almost homophonic (or chordal) in style; think of each bar as being just one chord. Block out the chords, as shown below, and practice moving smoothly from one chord to the next paying careful attention to the fingering.

Next, play the notes as written using a lateral wrist motion (where the wrist moves flexibly from side to side, *not* up and down). This technique helps to create an even tone, and supports the weaker fifth finger as it plays the top notes.

Try playing an accent with your fifth finger (in the right hand) as you practice (for example, on the G in the first bar (beat 1); although this must be omitted when performing, it can strengthen weaker fingers and help avoid the temptation to rush. The sixteenth note (semiquaver) patterns can be *legato*, but the last beat in each bar is more effective if played non-*legato*, bouncing off the left hand's eighth note (quaver).

Left-hand practice

The left hand can also be blocked out to aid practice. When playing the notes as written, ensure the first quarter note (crotchet) of each bar is given its full value, and always be aware of the rests.

Place a slight emphasis on the first beat of each bar, particularly in passages where a leap is required (for example, bars 22 and 23). Work at these, locating each jump carefully with a quick lateral wrist motion. Isolate each one and practice landing on each bass note much quicker than necessary.

Hands together

Work at four bars at a time with both hands together, blocking out the chords as before. Once the notes are under the fingers, it's important to ensure the pulse and rhythms are even. Counting in sixteenth notes (semiquavers) throughout will help.

Avoid rushing the last beat of each bar. Start by practicing this slowly and *legato*. As the speed increases, aim to produce a crisp, non-*legato* fourth beat providing the upbeat into the succeeding bars.

Always practice over the barline for continuity (for example, bars 19–20):

INTERPRETATION

Use dynamics to add drama and colour. Passages with added chromaticisms (notes which are not in the key signature), such as bars 22–28 can be played with more intensity and volume. Keep your wrist flexible, and use the weight of your arm to produce a warm sound.

Prelude in C minor

BWV 999

J.S. Bach (1685–1750)

Suggested tempo: ♩ = 88–92

Play it again: Piano – Book 1

Study in F major

Henry Lemoine (1786–1854)

This exciting study aims to strengthen the fingers by featuring lots of scale passages. It makes the fourth finger work particularly hard!

Set up

Key: F major
Time signature: ¢
Tempo: Allegro moderato
♩ = 112
Style: Early Romantic
Piano technique:

- Evenness: scale passages
- Control: strengthening the fourth finger

PREPARATION

Finger warm-up

Use the following exercise to warm-up the fingers and to prepare the fourth finger especially. This study is made up of patterns of sixteenth notes (semiquavers), which can cause tension in the hands if played over an extended period. This exercise can also help to control tension in the arm and wrist.

- The music example below uses the same note patterns and fingering as used in the study.
- Strike a note, playing deep into the key bed to produce a powerful sound, then drop the wrist.
- Keeping the note depressed, completely relax your hand, wrist and arm after the note has been played, making sure there is no tension.
- Repeat this technique for each note.
- Accent the fourth finger, used on the first note of each four-note pattern; this will help strengthen it.
- Play on the fingertips, with all finger joints fully engaged (not collapsing), ensuring 'hooked' fingers, using the wrist and hand flexibly.

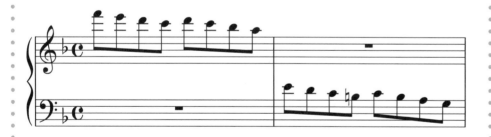

PRACTICE TECHNIQUES

Right-hand practice

Using the exercise on the previous page, work through bars 1–6 and 15–16 of the right hand. Listen carefully from the beginning to the end of each note; the end of a note is as vital as the start. Begin by working through a note at a time, then play in groups of four.

Aim to break the tension at the end of each group by stopping for a second, relaxing hand and arm muscles, as follows:

After a while, these breaks can become less frequent (say, every few bars), as muscles become more flexible and accustomed to feeling relaxed whilst playing groups of notes at speed.

Left-hand practice

Apply this same technique to bars 9–14. Extended patterns such as this will require a flexible wrist in order to move quickly and freely to the next note. This is especially true of bars 13–14 in the left-hand sixteenth note passagework where the hand must turn from C to F♯ repeatedly.

Hands together

When ready, put the hands together playing slowly and gradually increasing the speed. The metronome may prove useful here.

INTERPRETATION

Aim for each note to be clear and crisp. The accompanying chords must be very light and well-coordinated, providing shape and structure to the action in the other hand.

Study in F major

Op. 37 No. 20

Henry Lemoine (1786–1854)

Allegro moderato ♩ = 112

Play it again: Piano – Book 1

D.C. al Fine

Les Pifferari (The Italian Pipers)

Charles Gounod (1818–1893)

This lively piece is through-composed and its texture consists of a melody and accompaniment.

Set up

Key: F major
Time signature: 6/8
Tempo: Allegro ♩.= 120
Style: Romantic
Piano technique:
- Finger agility: scale passages
- Expression: characterisation and dynamics

PREPARATION

Warm up the fingers by playing through the scale and arpeggio of F major (page 29).

Block out each half-bar to start with; this can be done with hands separately at first, and then together. Work through the fingering then play all the notes for each dotted quarter note (crotchet) beat as a chord, like this:

Bars 6–9

This will help you to learn the note patterns, when and where they occur, and will also make you aware of the necessary movements needed to play them. The whole piece can be worked at in this manner.

PRACTICE TECHNIQUES

Right-hand practice
Take particular care over the articulation and phrasing. The fingering will help you achieve this, for example in bars 7–11, where the frequent hand-position changes encourage the fingers to leave the keyboard, making time for the rests in-between each note. Resist the urge to skip or rush these rests, as they contribute to the necessary character.

Use a 'drop roll' technique to keep the melody part flowing. This is where the hand and wrist sink down into the key as a note is played, and roll upwards on the next note, lifting off cleanly at the end of the second note (see page 30 for more information about this technique).

The scale passages need firm fingers; practice by playing each note with a full tone, pressing the fingertips down into the key bed.

The melody line has a dance-like feel rather like a jig. This requires a strict sense of pulse; always start by practicing at a third of the intended speed, and take care not to rush. Aim for a bouncy, jaunty melody with a slight leaning on the first eighth note (quaver) beat of each dotted quarter note.

Tip

Work at scale passages in isolation, practicing with various accents (on different fingers) and particular touches (such as *staccato*, *legato* or *non-legato*), in order to achieve rhythmic and tonal evenness. It can be helpful to try contrasting dynamics on rapid passagework too.

Left-hand practice
The left-hand chords are similar throughout, and each contains a middle C played by the thumb. Make sure that the lowest note of the chord is given greater emphasis, as this is effectively a secondary melody line. This will mean transferring the weight of your hand to the weaker fourth and fifth fingers, and away from the stronger thumb (which you want to play lightly). Try joining every chord to produce a smooth *legato* tone.

Hands together
Practice hands together slowly, increasing the speed accordingly. The outer notes of the chords play the melody, so these must be clearly heard. Isolate these, and decide how you are going to shape and colour the melody before you add the soft, accompanying inner parts of the chords.

INTERPRETATION
Gounod uses a wide range of dynamics, from *f* to *ppp*. Think about adding these at the earliest opportunity; they are a vital part of the piece's characterisation, and it's easier to build them in during the early stages of learning. Take care to add the accents in the left hand from the beginning. Be sure to add the pause on the last chord. The sustaining pedal will be effective if used on chordal passages (such as bars 37–48), but must be employed sparingly during scalic figurations.

Tip

'*Simile*' (in bar 8) instructs the player to continue a particular phrasing, articulation, pedalling or perhaps a dynamic gesture. In this case, the accents on the left hand chords should continue throughout the piece, probably phasing out with the *diminuendo* from bar 39.

Les Pifferari

The Italian Pipers

Charles Gounod (1818–1893)

Prelude in A major

Fryderyk Chopin (1810–1849)

This beautiful miniature is only 16 bars long, consisting of two 8-bar phrases. It has a chordal texture, and its ($\frac{3}{4}$) time signature creates a gently lilting character.

Set up

Key: A major
Time signature: $\frac{3}{4}$
Tempo: Andantino ♩= 80
Style: Romantic
Piano technique:
- *Legato* playing: moving from chord to chord
- Even tone: balancing the notes of the chord

PREPARATION

Start by practicing the A major scale and arpeggio. Familiarise yourself with the hand positions needed to incorporate the three sharps (F, C and G) and memorize the fingering and note patterns. Keep hands and wrists flexible and use a larger hand turn when approaching the skips of the arpeggio.

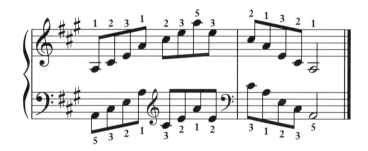

Tip

The sustain pedal will help you to achieve a *legato* sound; however, *legato* is accomplished more effectively and evenly when controlled by the fingers.

PRACTICE TECHNIQUES

Right-hand practice
Break the right hand down into two-bar segments and tackle them a section at a time. Pay careful attention to the *legato* fingering in order to create an even and balanced sound when moving from chord to chord.

Legato finger-work exercise

- Isolate the first group of three chords. Follow the suggested fingering; this may feel awkward at first but it will help achieve a *legato* sound.

- Each note in the chord should be voiced and balanced. Play the chords at several different volumes, from *fortissimo* to *pianissimo*, ensuring the notes sound together. To do this, press down on the keys and find the point in the key bed where the sound occurs. Note that the slower the attack, the softer the sound.
- Work through each bar balancing the chords in this way, moving slowly from chord to chord and observing the changing note patterns.

Highlighting the melody

- First, play just the tune using the correct fingering before adding the chords.
- Practice balancing the hand and wrist by tilting them slightly to the right and away from the body – this will support the weaker (4th and 5th) fingers and help bring the melody out over the other notes in the chord, even though they are played by the stronger fingers.
- Aim to play the top notes with a deeper, more focused sound.

Left-hand practice

Work at the left hand in bite-sized sections. The first beat of each bar should be stronger as it provides the base of the harmony; the remaining chords should be lighter and evenly balanced. Isolate the jumps; play them much quicker than intended keeping your arm light and flexible. At first, practice landing on the note without actually playing it, gauging the feeling and distance.

Hands together

Isolate each chordal progression, as seen here in bars 13–14.

Ensure the chords sound together and the top notes ring out, bringing out the melody. The chord at bar 12 can be negotiated by playing both the two lower notes with the thumb (a C♯ and A♯). If this is uncomfortable, play the A♯ with the left hand, spreading the whole chord across both hands from bottom to top with a rippled or arpeggiated effect, using the sustain pedal to catch the bass notes.

Use the sustain pedal at the beginning of each musical phrase (usually lasting 2 bars), releasing it just before the upbeat (or third beat of the bar) at the beginning of the next phrase.

Tip

To feel flexible and relaxed whilst playing chords, the wrist must be supple, allowing the hands and fingers to spread out and manage the notes in tandem.

INTERPRETATION

Add a slight 'push' or *tenuto* on the first strong beat of each phrase (after the upbeat). Although essentially gentle (or *dolce*, 'sweet'), this piece is all about pianistic colour, so once the notes are in place explore as many different dynamics as possible, building to the climactic point at bars 11–12.

Prelude in A major

Op. 28 No. 7

Fryderyk Chopin (1810–1849)

© 2017 Schott Music Ltd, London

202542

The Sailor's Hornpipe

Traditional, arranged by Barrie Carson Turner (b. 1951)

Set up

Key: G major
Time signature: 2/2
Tempo: Bright Tempo ♩= 112
Style: Folk/World
Piano technique:
- Tonal clarity
- Articulation

This arrangement of a popular traditional tune features two repeated sections with a coda. The texture is melody with accompaniment.

PREPARATION
Play through the G major scale and arpeggio (page 16) to familiarise yourself with the key of this piece.

PRACTICE TECHNIQUES
Right-hand practice
The melody should be played *legato*; in order to achieve this, however, the fingers will need to complete many twists and turns so it is important to use the correct fingering.

Finger-twisters!

- In the example above, the fingering has been added to the first three bars. Play the passage extremely slowly, making a powerful, full sound.

- Ensure your wrist is relaxed when moving your thumb under your second finger on the first two eighth notes (quavers) of bar 2.

- When practicing slowly, try making larger, exaggerated wrist movements when the fingers are moving under or over the hand; this can help to keep the hand relaxed and flexible. When the tempo is increased, the movements will become smaller but the hand-turns will be fluid and even.

Exaggerated movements will also help in passages such as bar 9, where good rotational movement in the wrist will help to keep the rhythm crisp and will enable the fifth finger to produce a full, even tone on the top notes.

Roll from thumb to 5th finger using the wrist, moving left to right

Practice Notes continue on page 76

The Sailor's Hornpipe

Traditional arr. Barrie Carson Turner (b. 1951)

© 2017 Schott Music Ltd, London

from **English Folk Tunes for Piano** by Barrie Carson Turner, Schott ED 13619

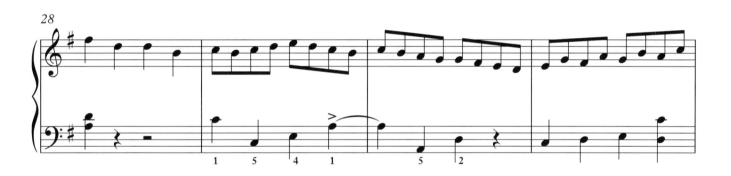

Left-hand practice

The left hand provides the accompaniment to the right-hand melody, so keep it understated throughout. The only exceptions are at bars 25–26, 27–28, 33–34 and 35–36, where the chords will require a fuller, non-*legato* sound.

Hands together

When putting both hands together, set the metronome to a slow speed and practice playing the eighth notes (quavers) extremely evenly and rhythmically. Divide the piece into four-bar phrases and work through a phrase at a time.

Aim for good coordination between the two hands; this may appear simple at first, but when playing at speed, passages such as the last line of the piece (below) will benefit from slow, exaggerated practice.

INTERPRETATION

Make good use of dynamics to add variety throughout the piece, especially in the repeats, and to keep a bright and interesting sound.

Mississippi Rag

John Kember (b. 1935)

Set up

Key: C major
Time signature: 2/4
Tempo: Ragtime ♩ = 69
Style: Contemporary
Piano technique:
- Rhythm: Ragtime syncopation

Mississippi Rag is set in four-bar phrases with a melody and accompaniment texture. The theme is stated twice, and is framed by a brief introduction and a coda.

PREPARATION

Revisit the key of C major and play through the scale and arpeggio (page 26), which by now should be familiar and comfortable. One particularly vital element in any rag is the rhythm, so it's important to keep an accurate pulse. Count evenly, in eighth notes (quavers), even adding this as numerals into the score; every note must be placed accurately within the pulse.

Keeping time

- A helpful technique for keeping time is to tap each hand's rhythm on the piano lid. This allows you to focus just on the rhythm, and will help you to keep a regular pulse.
- Start slowly and work up to the final tempo.
- Aim to have the rhythms familiarised before learning the notes.

PRACTICE TECHNIQUES

Right-hand practice
There are many hand-position changes throughout this piece which will require you to move quickly and flexibly. These can be tricky, so isolate them and work through any problem corners before thinking about the musical content.

Ties are an important part of the ragtime style, and create its characteristic off-beat or syncopated feel. The ties which appear on the last sixteenth note (semiquaver) of the first beat of the bar (for example in all of bars 1–4), must be carefully observed and counted. In order to prepare for these, it can be helpful to give a very slight accent or 'push' on the first note of each tied pair (for example the Cs in bar 1, 4th sixteenth note).

Left-hand practice
Both hands play the introduction in unison, and thereafter the left hand provides the accompaniment to the right hand's melody. The left hand may need work, so that it can keep up with the often more nimble right hand; experiment by practicing the left hand at different speeds and with various touches. Then with hands together, play the left hand *staccato* and right hand *legato*, for example, and then swap these touches around; try this process with dynamic changes and unusual accents too, in place of the *legato* and *staccato*.

Two-part pattern

- Practice the two-part pattern from bars 3–5 separately.

- Take the lower part and work out the fingering. Ensure the quarter note (crotchets) are even and *legato*.

- In contrast the upper part should be crisp and cleanly articulated; avoid playing the notes too heavily.

- Once each part has been mastered, combine them, making sure the lower line is smooth and audible and the upper part is in the background.

Hands together

The introduction demands perfect coordination. To achieve this, play slowly and deeply into the keys on the tips of your fingers and listen from the beginning to the end of each note; this is the best way to detect any notes which are not entirely together.

Slow practice will also be required for bars 7–9, and all similar passages, in order for the fingers to work through the three separate parts (two in the left hand and one in the right).

INTERPRETATION

Keep the sound bright and bold, with contrasting dynamics and a vibrant, penetrating touch. The left-hand passages at bars 6, 10 and 18 would be enhanced by an increase in the sound leading onto the next phrase.

Mississippi Rag

John Kember (b. 1935)

from **Ragtime** by John Kember, Schott ED 12890

Three 'Outasight' Mice

Bill Readdy (b. 1953)

This piece, enriched with blues and jazz harmonies, consists of four-bar phrases and a melody and accompaniment texture.

Set up

Key: C major
Time signature: 6/8
Tempo: Lento, rubato con molto espressione ♩. = 63
Style: Contemporary/Jazz
Piano technique:
- *Legato* chords
- Expression: playing in a blues style

PREPARATION

Play through the scale and arpeggio of C major (page 26) as a warm-up. However, be aware that this work is built around chromatic blues inflections which are only loosely based on the home key.

PRACTICE TECHNIQUES

Right-hand practice

Start by working through the various note patterns, taking a bar at a time. Block out the notes of each dotted quarter note (crotchet) beat and aim to work through the piece like this – one hand at a time, and then with hands together. Below is an example of this technique applied to bars 13–16.

This piece should be played with a *legato* touch, so work through one four-bar phase at a time making sure your fingers are joining notes together as much as possible. Some sliding between notes will be necessary – creating the illusion of *legato* – like this (bars 5–7):

Try to keep a firm (but slow) pulse when practicing, and enjoy the chromatic harmonies. Ensure the top note rings out above the rest of the chordal texture.

Left-hand practice

The left hand's accompanying eighth notes (quavers) should be light and soft. Many of the eighth note patterns require a stretch of over an octave, so use a flexible wrist and relaxed hand to reach the notes. Encourage the hand to move generously from one note to the next, so that you join the notes in a *legato* manner, with no gap in the sound; this is particularly important where there are larger intervals such as those in bars 7, 18, 21, 22, 24, 25, 26, 27 and 31.

Tip

Make each tempo change carefully, adding tasteful rubato where marked, capturing the mood.

Hands together

When first playing with both hands together, try blocking out each beat to help tackle the note patterns. Be sure to hold the long notes right to the end of the bar.

Repeated notes

This exercise will help when practicing a series of *legato* repeated notes, such as the repeated Gs in bars 9–14. These should be played softly and evenly with the fifth finger.

- Depress each G slowly, so that it sounds very quietly.
- Hold the note down until the very last moment before replaying. Then as quickly as possible, replay the note, taking it down again without 'hitting' it; caress the note, balancing the sound so each G is barely audible, allowing the first of each group of three eighth notes to be slightly more prominent.
- If this is done neatly and quickly, there shouldn't be any gaps in the sound between each note.

Rhythm: 'Three-against-two'

Bars 15–16 feature a 'three-against-two' rhythm: the right hand plays two notes against the three eighth notes in the left hand.

- Play this very slowly at first.
- Place the second right-hand note (B♭) firmly between the C and the E in the left hand.
- Make sure the left hand's eighth notes are even at all times.

The last two bars could be divided between the hands as in the following example. Keep the sustaining pedal depressed for the duration (across both bars).

INTERPRETATION

Acciaccaturas may be played in a slightly lazy fashion, in-keeping with the blues character of the music.

The tempo changes which feature throughout the piece capture the character of the mischievous mice. Practice in tempo until confident, and then experiment with the suggested **rallentandos** (gradual slowing down). Aim for a laid-back, free, very expressive performance when playing *Three 'Outasight' Mice*.

Three 'Outasight' Mice

Bill Readdy (b. 1953)

Lento, rubato con molto espressione ♩. = 63

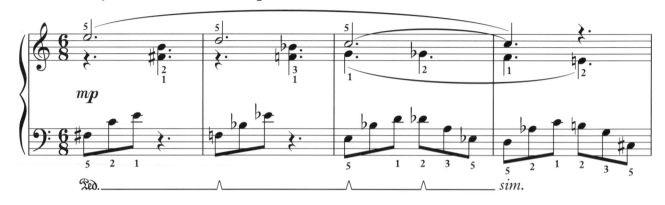

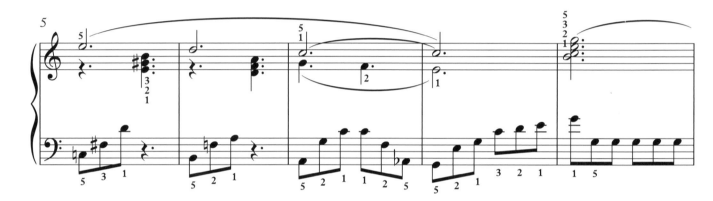

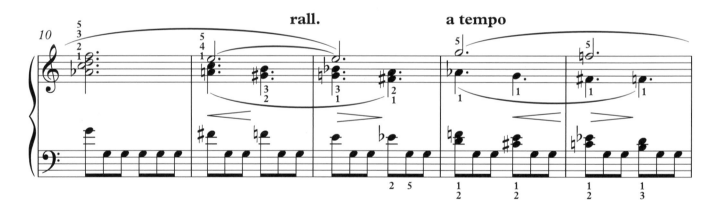

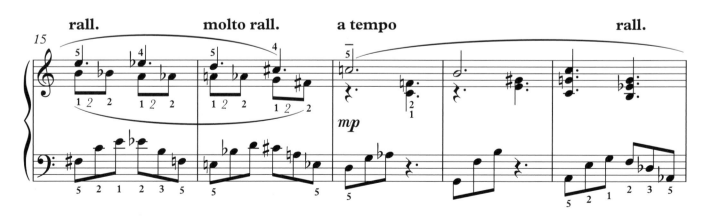

from **Jazz It** by Bill Readdy, Schott ED 12728

a tempo

molto rall.

very slow

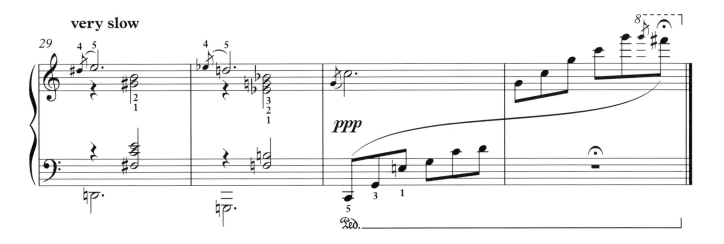

Intermediate
Sonatina in G major
Muzio Clementi (1752–1832)

This is the first movement of a **sonatina** *(or small sonata: an instrumental piece generally containing two to four movements in related keys). It is set in* **sonata form** *with three distinct sections.*

Set up
Key: G major
Time signature: $\frac{2}{4}$
Tempo: Allegretto ♩ = 96
Style: Classical
Piano technique:
- Articulation: phrasing, slurs and *staccato*
- Tonal and rhythmic control: sixteenth note (semiquaver) passagework

PREPARATION
Start by practicing hand turns, which are very common in the right hand in this piece.

Hand-turns exercise
- Isolate passages and work on them carefully, such as the example below from bars 15–16. There are three turns highlighted here:

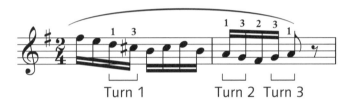

Turn 1   Turn 2 Turn 3

- Play each sixteenth note (semiquaver) slowly, allowing the wrist to flop loosely after every note, so it feels very relaxed, but the finger is still depressing the key. This will enable the hand to turn without any tension or stiffness.

- Use large movements to begin with and, when confident, add speed using a lighter touch and smaller hand movements. The slow practice will aid flexibility and agility, helping create an even touch.

PRACTICE TECHNIQUES
Right-hand practice
The articulation of the melody has been clearly annotated. Each phrase mark or slur will require a 'drop roll' motion (see page 30), and each *staccato* marking should be played with a slight lift, as opposed to a very short stab, creating elegant eighth notes (quavers) and encouraging each note to be part of the larger phrase.

Observe the suggested dynamic markings including the **sforzando** (to play suddenly with force) on the first beat of bar 2. Extended sixteenth note passagework, such as at bars 19–22, will benefit from very slow practice, using a heavy, powerful touch, ensuring every note is completely even and rhythmical. Count in small subdivisions for accuracy and precision; try counting in sixteenth notes or even thirty-second notes (demisemiquavers) .

Tip

Supporting the fifth finger
As the fifth finger plays the sixteenth note (semiquaver) top As in bars 20 and 21, move your wrist very slightly to the right; this will support the finger and help to make a full sound equal to that of the other fingers, allowing the whole passage to be tonally and rhythmically even. It will also stop the urge either to rush the notes by not sounding them fully, or slow down by lingering too long.

Some finger changes will need care, such as at the beginning of bar 3; the closer to the keys the fingers are, the quicker and smoother such changes will be.

Left-hand practice
The left hand alternates between a *legato* and *staccato* accompaniment, punctuated with scale passages and chords. The *legato* passages (for example, in bars 1–6) can be blocked out for ease of learning and then played very smoothly and evenly. The *staccato* passages (for example, bars 7–9) should be played with a non-*legato* touch as opposed to very short stabbing sounds, in-keeping with the Classical style.

Octaves

When tackling octaves (for example, bars 8–9), slowly extend the hand and drop the wrist to keep it relaxed. Make sure your fifth finger 'stands' rather than lies flat across the note as shown in the photo; only when this feels free of tension should you start playing *staccato*.

Hands together
Good coordination is essential when playing with hands together. It may take some practice to achieve the correct articulation in both the left and right hands. In bar 7, for example, the *staccato* chords in the left hand and the *legato* sixteenth notes in the right hand will need to be thoroughly learnt hands separately and worked at slowly so that they become second nature. The rapid broken chords at bar 12 must be 'placed' rhythmically; avoid rushing onto the chords in the following bar, count carefully and take time for all notes to sound clearly.

Tip

It can be useful to practice an eighth note (quaver) beat at a time, playing, for example, a left hand chord such as bar 7, beat 2, staccato, combined with the two corresponding *legato* sixteenth notes (semiquavers) in the right hand (D and C♯). Experiment by reversing the *staccato* and *legato* between the hands. Now add accents to the right-hand part, then to the left, and finally work with various dynamics. This constant variation between the hands encourages the brain to become accustomed to challenging coordination.

INTERPRETATION
Avoid using the sustain pedal so that the finger work and articulation are kept clean, clear and beautifully phrased. The ends of phrases can be tapered off (for example, in the right hand of bar 14, and over the barline between bars 43–44).

Sonatina in G major

Op. 36 No.2

Muzio Clementi (1752–1832)

Study in C Major

Carl Czerny (1791–1857)

This fast-paced study features rapid scale figurations which are passed between the hands; perfect for strengthening the fingers, and developing good hand coordination.

Set up

Key: C major
Time signature: 𝄴
Tempo: Allegro molto ♩= 160
Style: Early Romantic
Piano technique:
- Finger and hand coordination: sixteenth note (semiquaver) passagework

PREPARATION

Play through the C major scale and arpeggio (page 26) to warm-up the fingers and familiarise yourself with the key of this piece.

Rhythm plays an important role in this study, so it may be helpful to tap the rhythm using both hands before tackling the notes, ensuring that the interplay between the hands is tight and precise. Work at two bars at a time.

PRACTICE TECHNIQUES

Right-hand practice
Aim for sixteenth note (semiquaver) passages to be played evenly and with crisp articulation. Using the suggested fingering will help with this. To develop strong and independent fingers, play deeply into the key bed on the tips of your fingers. Play slowly, *legato*, and with a powerful sound at first, then play with a lighter touch making sure to pick the fingers up cleanly after each note. You should hopefully hear evenly articulated notes.

Left-hand practice
The left hand takes the lead in this study. By aiming for clean finger work and even articulation the whole piece will fall into place. The left hand can often feel like the weaker hand, so its sixteenth note passages may need a little more work. For clarity, try playing bars 1–5 at different octaves, listening to each sixteenth note run, ensuring equality.

Fourth finger exercise

The fourth finger starts many of the runs, and should feel more comfortable after practicing this exercise:

- Oscillate between the C and D to an eighth note (quaver) then sixteenth note (semiquaver) pattern, playing with a full sound and relaxing and dropping the wrist between each note.
- Add accents to alternating notes in the pattern; first to all the Cs and then to the Ds. Playing *staccato* and non-*legato* can help fingers attain independence too.
- Gradually increase the speed and finger power. This exercise will help to strengthen the fingers but requires slow, careful work so as to not damage or strain any finger. Only practice this exercise for very short periods of time.

Hands together
In order to play runs seamlessly and in groups of four, try adding accents, like this (bars 3 and 4):

You don't need to add these accents when the fingers are working smoothly, but they provide shape and definition when the hands first play together.

Ghost practicing

'Ghost' practicing can be a useful tool. It requires complete concentration, but can be an excellent way to learn the notes and rhythm patterns.

It works by practicing with one hand alone on the keyboard, whilst imagining playing the other hand. For example, play the first four notes of the left hand in bar 3, and 'hear' (but don't play) the next four notes played by the right hand. Then continue playing the left hand on beat three.

INTERPRETATION
Czerny is very exact about dynamics, with *crescendo* and *diminuendo* markings occurring within the space of one bar (for example, bars 1 and 2). Aim for swift changes from *piano* to *forte* for a colourful and exciting performance.

Study in C Major

Op. 849 No. 29

Carl Czerny (1791–1857)

Ballade in C minor

Johann Friedrich Franz Burgmüller (1806–1874)

Set up

Key: C minor
Time signature: 3/8
Tempo: Allegro con brio
♪. = 104
Style: Romantic
Piano technique:

- Keeping a steady pulse
- Left-hand agility: playing the melody in the left hand
- Coordination: finger strength

This Romantic work offers the opportunity for plenty of colour and drama.

PREPARATION

Developing finger strength

Bars 87–90 are probably the most challenging of the piece. This exercise shows you how to break them down and practice whilst developing finger strength and coordination.

- Work through the notes with separate hands to begin with, playing powerfully with the tips of your fingers.
- Once both hands are secure, play again but with the following rhythm patterns:

- Practice many different combinations of rhythm, touch and dynamics similar to the suggested exercise above. The more variations you try, the easier the coordination will feel, and the deeper into the keys you play, the stronger your fingers will become. Once you have practiced this slowly for some time, lighten your touch and add speed.

PRACTICE TECHNIQUES

Right-hand practice
The right hand's *staccato* chords will need a light touch and perfect coordination for all the notes to sound together. Aim to relax the wrist completely after each bar. To practice this, create a slight gap or break between the bars to begin with to free your hand and wrist (giving it a rest from the repeated chord shape). Gradually reduce the gap until your wrist is used to the quick movement and doesn't 'lock up' after several bars of the same action.

The middle section (bars 31–56) in C major provides sunny relief from the minor key, and a chance to use a cantabile touch. Play using the pads of your fingers, and keep your wrist flexible.

Practice Notes continue on page 94

Ballade in C minor

Op. 100 No. 15

Johann Friedrich Franz Burgmüller (1806–1874)

Play it again: Piano – Book 1

Left-hand practice

The melody is in the left hand during the outer sections. Use the fourth finger exercise on page 88 as preparation for this passagework. Try accenting the fourth and fifth sixteenth notes (semiquavers). Use your wrist flexibly, encouraging it to move freely, supporting the weaker fingers (such as the 4th) as you play, alleviating any tension.

Tip

Sforzando *sfz* (at bars 7, 9, 15 and 17) indicates a sudden surge in sound on a particular note, here adding drama.

The left hand plays accompanying chords during the middle section. Play just one chord in each bar, heavily, until you are sure of the chord changes and fingerings. Once secure, lighten your touch and play two chords in each bar as written.

Hands together

The pulse must remain constant throughout this work. A metronome can help with practice (set to a sixteenth note (semiquaver) or eighth note (quaver) beat). Resist the urge to clip the last beat of the bar, especially in those with sixteenth notes.

Unusual accents

Practicing by deliberately displacing the usual accents is a great way to develop coordination. When the correct accents are put back in, coordination will feel much more comfortable.

- Try accenting the off-beats in the following section of the left hand:

- Then add the following accents to the right hand:

INTERPRETATION

Add the sustaining pedal to the chords at bars 28–30 and 84–86, and to the final chord. This piece is all about dynamic variation, therefore aim to create drama and colour with quick, atmospheric changes.

A Little Night Music

Wolfgang Amadeus Mozart (1756–1791), arranged by Hans-Günter Heumann (b. 1955)

Set up

Key: G major
Time signature: 4/4
Tempo: Allegro ♩ = 112
Style: Classical
Piano technique:
- Articulation: rests, slurs and *staccato*
- Coordination: playing in unison

This is an arrangement of a Mozart favourite for string ensemble. It conveys the character effectively with a clear melody and accompaniment texture.

PREPARATION

Arpeggios

Play through the following exercise to prepare for the piece's arpeggios.

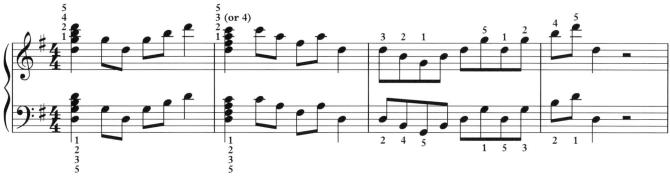

- Practice with hands separately and then together, sticking to the suggested fingering.

- Blocking out the note patterns as chords may also be helpful (as in bars 1 and 2 of this example).

- Play *legato* to begin with, moving on to staccato only when the hand positions are secure.

Tip

Play with your fingertips and keep your fingers close to the keys for more precise playing.

PRACTICE TECHNIQUES

Right-hand practice

Work on the *staccato* passages a section at a time. Practice these sections (such as the opening four bars) at a quarter of the intended speed; keep the wrist and hand flexible and mobile between every note, with your fingers close to the keys. Use circular wrist movements between notes to keep the wrist flexible. Once you are confident, increase the speed.

Follow the precise articulation notated in the score: slurs and *staccato* notes (such as those in bars 5–7) add colour, punctuation and character to this piece.

Practice Notes continue on page 98

A Little Night Music

Allegro *from* **Serenade in G Major, KV 525**

Wolfgang Amadeus Mozart (1756–1791)
arr. Hans-Günter Heumann (b. 1955)

© 2017 Schott Music Ltd, London
from **A Little Night Music** by Hans-Günter Heumann, Schott ED 13485

96 Play it again: Piano – Book 1

Left-hand practice
Repeated chords feature prominently in the left hand, imitating the
orchestral texture. These passages would be played by lower stringed
instruments in Mozart's original version.

Repeated movements such as this can create tension in the wrist, so
practice 'bouncing' between the chords (moving the wrist up and down
like a hinge), keeping the sound light and rhythmic.

Hands together
The hands play in rhythmic unison in the opening four bars, so good
coordination is vital here. To practice this, experiment by adding
accents on the irregular beats:

When practicing bars 5–8, start by playing very slowly and *legato*,
ensuring fingers are completely coordinated before working on the
articulation and increasing the speed.

For a successful performance, the piece must have a steady pulse
throughout. Learn to rely on your sense of pulse and count aloud in
sixteenth notes (semiquavers) for accuracy.

INTERPRETATION
Keep use of the sustaining pedal to an absolute minimum, using it
simply to add resonance at the ends of phrases.

Adhere to rest signs scrupulously as they give the music a sense
of space, lightness and time to breathe.

Gymnopédie No. 1

Erik Satie (1866–1925)

Set up

Key: D major

Time signature: 𝄴 3/4

Tempo: Lent et douloureux
♩ = 76

Style: Impressionist /
Late Romantic

Piano technique:

- Touch and colour: playing in
  a *cantabile* style

This popular piece is all about colour and creating an atmospheric sound world.

PREPARATION

This piece contains three distinct layers of texture (from bars 5–8):
The melody (in the right hand):

The accompaniment (notated as chords in the bass clef but if necessary shared between the hands):

The bass or bottom of the harmony (in the left hand):

Each line requires a different colour or timbre; start by identifying each part, and perhaps mark them in the score.

PRACTICE TECHNIQUES

Left-hand practice

Start with the bass notes; locate them and decipher the fingering. Then practice the chords in the middle of the texture which will pass between the right and left hands (the larger chords beginning in bar 24 might need both hands). Play them evenly, and ensure all the notes of the chord sound at the same time.

Putting the bass notes and chords together

Playing the bass notes and chords at the same time might appear challenging, but very slow practice and quick light arm movements will help.

- After playing a bass note, move to the chord much quicker than is necessary. Aim to arrive at the chords half a beat early.
- Stop and rest on the notes, finding the correct hand position before playing.
- This practice should improve accuracy and avoid a last-minute panic to locate the notes.

Practice Notes continue on page 102

Gymnopédie No. 1

Erik Satie (1866–1925)

Playing chords larger than an octave

- Chords which stretch beyond an octave reach might challenge small hands; notes can either be omitted, or it may be possible for both hands to negotiate the stretches.
- Stretching must be done judiciously so as not to strain wrists and hands. Lay your hand flat over the intended notes (but don't play them – merely extend the fingers to cover the stretch) and completely relax the hand muscles. Make sure the wrist isn't too high. The trick is to relax the hand muscles whilst in the outstretched position, so it feels normal, natural and easy.
- If you work at this movement little and often, your stretch will extend and a reach of a ninth will feel comfortable.

Right-hand practice
Each of the right-hand chords in the opening four bars (notated on the lower stave) must sound together, with a soft, distant timbre. Begin by playing each chord powerfully so that the notes sound together, then gradually lighten your touch. Make sure the top notes (F♯) ring out above the other notes in the chord.

The melody starts from bar 5 and is noticeable for its use of long, continuous phrases. Once the notes and fingerings are secure, decide exactly where the tops of the phrases are going to be. The phrases are quite similar, so use dynamics to add variety. You might consider the following for the first part of the opening phrase, for example:

Use a *cantabile* touch for a deeper, fuller sound: play with the pads of the fingers to the bottom of the key bed, ensuring your arm and shoulder are relaxed, and encouraging a loose and flexible wrist to harness your arm weight.

Hands together
The piece requires you to think in three parts, which is why it is vital to know each part thoroughly. Slow practice will help develop good coordination. While this piece might appear full of *rubato* and *ritenuto*, in reality, it requires a steady pulse.

INTERPRETATION

This is primarily a quiet, soft piece; however, the right hand melody explores a variety of sonorities and colours. The final chords can be placed deliberately, bringing out the top notes, with a little *ritenuto*. The sustaining pedal can be used in every bar and generally held for the whole bar, creating a hazy, atmospheric effect.

Fried Chicken

Jürgen Moser (b. 1949)

Set up

Key: A major
Time signature: 4/4
Tempo: Not too fast ♩ = 156
Style: Contemporary/Rock
Piano technique:
- Rhythm: playing in a rock style

This lively rock piece is set around four-bar phrases and has a chordal texture.

PREPARATION

Play through the A major scale and arpeggio (page 70), then play all the notes of the arpeggio together as one chord (A, C♯, E and A). This pattern features heavily in *Fried Chicken*. To become accustomed to the octave stretch used in the right hand, gently rock from side to side from the thumb to the fifth finger. The wrist must rotate slowly and freely between the notes, supporting the fingers and encouraging a relaxed feeling in the whole arm.

PRACTICE TECHNIQUES

Left-hand practice
The left hand accompaniment needs a firm, strong sound to support the melody in the right hand.

Octaves

- Octaves feature throughout for the left hand. Aim to play them without any tension.
- Start by playing the bottom of the octaves from bar 4, usually with the fifth finger, playing on your fingertips.
- Work through all of the bass notes in this way; then play again lightly adding the top notes with the thumb.
- To avoid tension, drop your wrist, keeping it relaxed. A high wrist will prevent you from playing with speed and fluency.
- Play the two notes of the octave and, once they have sounded, let the wrist drop whilst holding the notes in position.
- Then move the wrist up and down freely (but still holding the keys down) before moving to the next chord.

Right-hand practice
The right hand features a series of **broken chords**; that is, with the notes of each chord played successively instead of all at once. Try blocking out the chords throughout the whole piece. For example, the first four bars would be blocked out like this:

Practice Notes continue on page 106

Fried Chicken

Jürgen Moser (b. 1949)

Not too fast ♩ = 156
(No Chords)

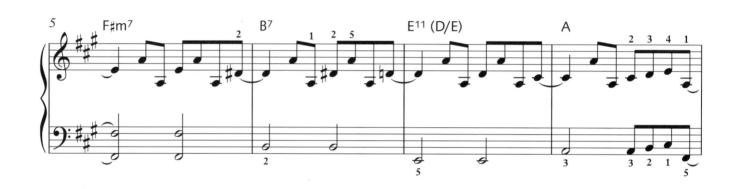

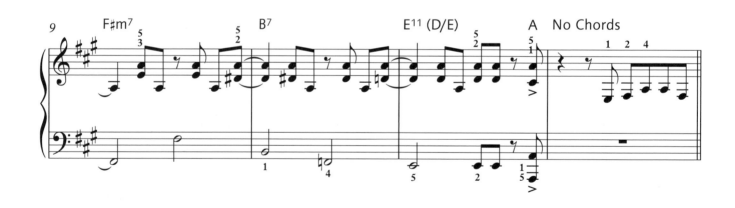

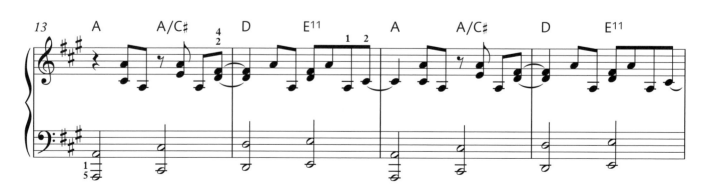

from **Discovering Rock Piano** by Jürgen Moser, Schott ED 13069

Play it again: Piano – Book 1

As the notes become more familiar, look at the rhythm, which features a recurring syncopation on the last eighth note (quaver) of the bar, tied to the first beat of the next; this is a quintessential feature of the rock style.

The right hand can almost be played in one position throughout, and this can result in tension building up in the arm and wrist if you're not careful. Keep your wrist and arm moving to avoid locking up.

Practicing hand turns

If you use the suggested fingering in the right hand at bar 22, a hand turn will be required in order to play in two different positions, one after another in quick succession smoothly. You could 'jump' here, but it's easier and more reliable to turn the hand. Try this exercise:

- After the thumb plays the A on the 3rd beat of the bar (the 5th finger should still be holding the E at this point), make a large hand turn over the thumb, releasing the 5th finger E but keeping the A depressed. Hold the fingers in position ready for the following E and A, and allow the hand, finger and thumb muscles to relax.

- Now practice playing the following E and A whilst holding down the thumb on the A. In effect you will only sound the E (with a 2nd finger), as the 5th finger will merely 'join' the thumb on the already depressed A. This allows you to feel the necessary movement in the hand and thumb joint, becoming aware of the muscles as they relax.

- Then, swiftly replace the thumb with the 5th finger on the A, this time ensuring the A sounds again and matches tonally, adding the lower E with the 2nd finger. Finally, complete the hand turn by moving the thumb out to a natural position (ready for the C♯ at the end of the bar). Once you have practiced this slowly, try it much faster than necessary, so that when you return to the correct tempo it should feel comfortable. Through careful and repeated practice of this movement, you will also easily achieve accuracy.

Hands together
Run through the piece at a quarter of the final speed, blocking out the various chordal progressions. Pay attention to the pulse throughout; the syncopations won't be as effective without precise counting.

INTERPRETATION
Use a bright, heavy touch with slightly detached notes in the right hand to create the piece's rock character.

Karma

Melanie Spanswick (b. 1969)

Set up

Key: E major
Time signature: 3/4
Tempo: Con moto ♩ = 132
Style: Minimalist/
Contemporary
Piano technique:
- Touch: playing in a *cantabile* style
- Tonal control: creating a smooth, even sound

Karma, from Digressions written in 2015, has a tuneful melody and is in the warm key of E major. It is set in ternary form (A-B-A) and has a melody and accompaniment texture.

PREPARATION

Work through the scale and arpeggio of E major – the key of this piece.

Take a moment to locate the key's four sharps (F♯, C♯, G♯ and D♯).

PRACTICE TECHNIQUES

Left-hand practice
A secure left hand is the key to playing this piece well; aim for a smooth and even sound. The patterns lie comfortably under the hand. Play powerfully into the key bed at first to produce a strong tone, then lighten your touch.

During the four bar introduction, and in bars 25–28, give a slight 'push' or accent on the first and third beats of the bar to highlight what is essentially the melody at these points.

Practice Notes continue on page 110

Karma

from **Digressions**

Melanie Spanswick (b. 1969)

Right-hand practice

Block out the short right-hand phrases (for example at bars 9–10 and 11–12) to learn the hand positions and fingering.

Now think about shaping each phrase according to the dynamic marking, with the sound generally rising to the top of each phrase before falling away.

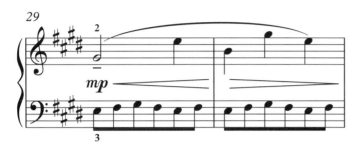

Hands together

Aim for a smooth *legato* sound throughout, with good coordination between the hands, an even tone and accurate rhythms. Play solidly at first, with strong fingers for a warm tone, then use a lighter tone as you increase the tempo. It may help to practice using accents on the 1st and 3rd beats of the bar, then on the 2nd beat, whilst you work at coordination.

Resist the urge to rush the last eighth note (quaver) in each bar, whether in the right or left hand (for example, the final F♯ in the left hand in bar 9, right); it's easy to do this when the note and rhythmic patterns are symmetrical and repetitive. A particular challenge will be to keep the left hand light whilst playing a *cantabile* melody. Balance between the hands relies on careful and intuitive listening, so attune your ears by reversing the dynamics (left hand *forte*, right hand *piano*).

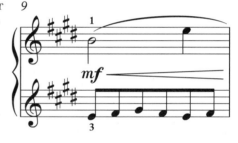

INTERPRETATION

Make good use of the sustaining pedal to add sonority. Pedal with the right-hand melody; this will require some deft footwork once playing at the intended speed.

Note the return of the rhythmic, repetitive pattern at bar 25, leading to the *fortissimo* climax. When the melody returns at bar 29, it should sound soft and distant but still with a rich tone. Play this melody with the pads rather than the tips of your fingers to create this sound.

The closing chords should be perfectly balanced with all the notes of each chord sounding together. Experiment to find out just how softly you can play these chords, making sure that each is quieter than the last, fading away at the end.

Basic reminders

This chapter can be revisited as many times as is necessary throughout Play it again 1 *and* 2, *providing the bedrock of music theory and notation.*

CLEFS AND STAVES

The treble clef and bass clef generally indicate that the pianist should use the right and left hand respectively.

The **stave** is the five lines on which the notes are written. There are two staves for piano music: the treble clef (or right-hand) stave is placed above the bass clef (or left-hand) stave.

Notes written in the treble clef are usually above middle C (although this is not always the case). The treble clef is sometimes called the G clef, as the sign curls around the G line (or second line of the stave).

The bass clef sits on the lower stave and its notes are generally written below middle C (but again, not always). The bass clef is sometimes called the F clef as the sign curls around the F line (or fourth line of the stave).

KEYBOARD AND NOTE LAYOUT

This chart illustrates the white keys at the centre of the piano keyboard, and their corresponding notes on the stave.

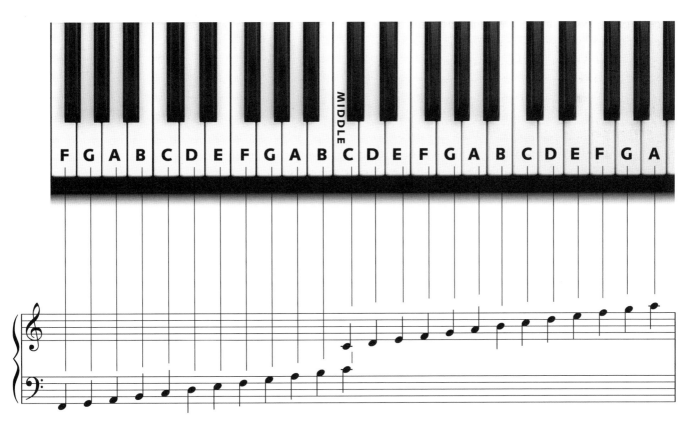

Notes which are too high or too low to be written within the staves are written above or below on extra lines known as **ledger lines** (see the top A here for an example of a ledger line).

Many piano tutor books begin by locating 'middle C', followed by all notes moving outwards from this point. You can find middle C on your piano more or less in the middle of the keyboard and to the left of a group of two black notes.

A gap or space between one note and another is known as an **interval**; a gap or interval of eight notes is called an **octave**, which looks like this on the stave:

In the example below, the notes in the right hand rise from middle C to the C an octave higher, and in the left hand, the notes fall from middle C to the C an octave lower:

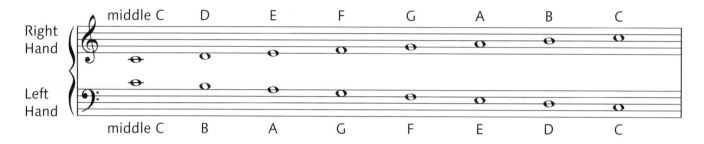

SHARPS, FLATS AND NATURALS

A **sharp** sign (♯) placed before a note on the score *raises* it by a **semitone** (or half step). A **flat** sign (♭) placed before a note on the score *lowers* it by a semitone.

A semitone is the shortest distance between two notes on the piano; the distance of two semitones is a **whole tone**.

The following example demonstrates how sharps, flats and naturals (♮ , where a note is returned to its 'normal' state) are displayed on a score.

Recap

Let's try a quick recap on note names:

- Look at the score below which features notes in various positions around the stave plus several notes on ledger lines.
- Begin by saying the name of each note in either clef (one clef at a time), then try to find them on the keyboard.
- Try this exercise during your practice sessions until you feel confident at finding notes with ease.

FINGERING

An important aspect of piano playing is fingering, determining which finger plays which note at any given time. Each finger has its own number, as shown here.

Aim to use the fingering indicated every time you practice. If fingering hasn't been written in, you will eventually be able to do it yourself as you become more aware of finger patterns and the geography of the keyboard.

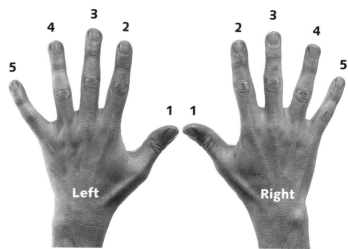

These numbers indicate which finger should be used to play which note.

RHYTHM: NOTE VALUES AND RESTS

When reading a note on a piano score, there is a three-part thought process; first, recognise the note, secondly, identify its location on the keyboard, and thirdly, determine how long the note should be held. Of course, as you develop, this three-part thought process will become increasingly natural and instantaneous.

The shape of a note indicates its 'value' (how long it should be held). For every note value, there is an equivalent rest (or a silence). The chart below shows how the main note values and their corresponding rests are written.

American and elsewhere	Shape	Rest	Value in terms of a whole note	British
Whole note	o		1	Semibreve
Half note			1/2	Minim
Quarter note			1/4	Crotchet
Eighth note			1/8	Quaver
Sixteenth note			1/16	Semiquaver
Thirty-second note			1/32	Demisemiquaver

The chart below illustrates the note values in relation to each other. In each case the value of a note is half that of the preceding note in the chart; for example, a half note (minim) is half the duration of a whole note (semibreve).

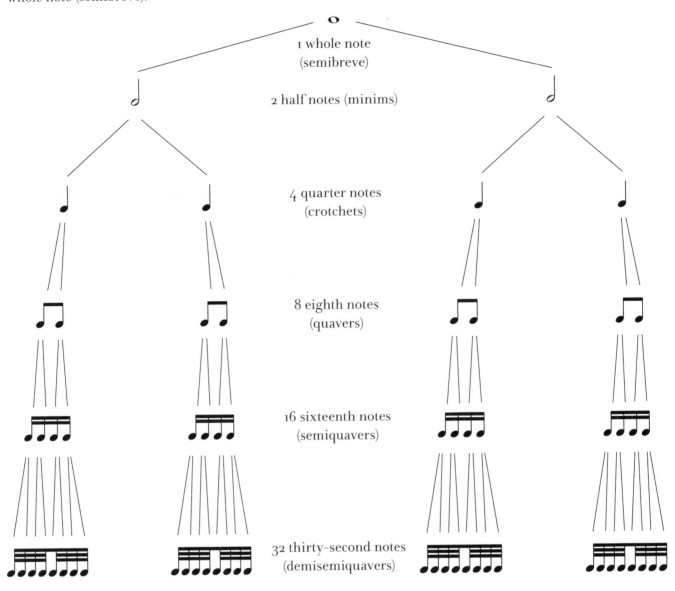

TIME SIGNATURES, BARS AND BARLINES

Bars contain a set number of beats and are separated by **barlines**. The **time signature**, written at the beginning of a piece of music, indicates the number of beats in each bar. They show two numbers: the top number tells us how many beats there are in every bar and the bottom number indicates the value of the beat, so a piece with a $\frac{2}{4}$ time signature will consist of two quarter note beats in each bar. A time signature of $\frac{6}{8}$ indicates six eighth note beats in each bar.

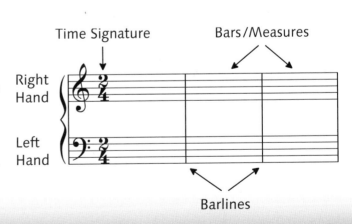

The following charts clarify the most frequently employed time signatures, which are either **simple** or **compound**, that is, with beats divided into either two or three main **subdivisions**.

SIMPLE TIME

	Duple Time Two beats in each bar	Triple Time Three beats in each bar	Quadruple Time Four beats in each bar
A quarter note (crotchet) = 1 beat/count	**2/4** ♩ ♩	**3/4** ♩ ♩ ♩	**4/4** ♩ ♩ ♩ ♩
A half note (minim) = 1 beat/count	**2/2** 𝅗𝅥 𝅗𝅥	**3/2** 𝅗𝅥 𝅗𝅥 𝅗𝅥	**4/2** 𝅗𝅥 𝅗𝅥 𝅗𝅥 𝅗𝅥
An eighth note (quaver) = 1 beat/count	**2/8** ♪ ♪	**3/8** ♪ ♪ ♪	**4/8** ♪ ♪ ♪ ♪

COMPOUND TIME

	Duple Time Two beats in each bar	Triple Time Three beats in each bar	Quadruple Time Four beats in each bar
A dotted quarter note = 1 beat/count	**6/8** ♩. ♩.	**9/8** ♩. ♩. ♩.	**12/8** ♩. ♩. ♩. ♩.
A dotted half note = 1 beat/count	**6/4** 𝅗𝅥. 𝅗𝅥.	**9/4** 𝅗𝅥. 𝅗𝅥. 𝅗𝅥.	**12/4** 𝅗𝅥. 𝅗𝅥. 𝅗𝅥. 𝅗𝅥.
A dotted eighth note = 1 beat/count	**6/16** ♪. ♪.	**9/16** ♪. ♪. ♪.	**12/16** ♪. ♪. ♪. ♪.

PULSE AND KEEPING TIME

Developing a feel for rhythm and how to keep a steady pulse is vital for good piano playing. Using a metronome (a mechanical device producing a regular ticking beat) to provide a background pulse can be very helpful.

In order to play you still need to know how long each note or rest lasts. Counting aloud and subdividing the beat is a very reliable method of developing a steady pulse. Subdividing involves splitting the main beat into two, three or four equal parts in order to count in smaller units.

Keeping the pulse

An effective way to learn note values, and to practice keeping time, is to do so away from the keyboard.

- Work through the following examples by tapping on your piano lid or a table top.
  Middle C has been used to denote the rhythm only.
- Practice slowly at first, feeling the pulse and coordinating your taps accordingly.
- Try to be absolutely even when counting, like the ticking of a clock.

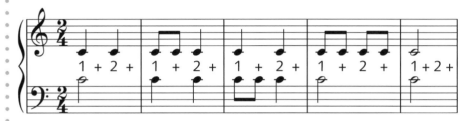

KEYS AND KEY SIGNATURES

A key signature is a set of sharp ($\sharp$) or flat ($\flat$) symbols placed together on the stave. It is placed just before the time signature. **Major** keys tend to have a bright, happy mood and **minor** keys tend to be used for music which is sad or dramatic in feeling. Every major key has a **relative minor** key, which shares the same key signature and can be found by counting three semitones down from the major, so C major's relative minor is A minor, and E major's is C$\sharp$ minor.

The example to the right shows the key of G major (or E minor), containing one sharp (F$\sharp$) shown in the treble and bass clef. The middle of the sharp sign is written on the F line of each stave.

In practical terms, there are 24 keys in Western music: 12 major and 12 minor, with each pair having its own set of sharps or flats (or none at all in the case of C major and A minor).